VALUING AN ENTREPRENEURIAL ENTERPRISE

VALUING AN
ENTREPRENEURIAL
ENTERPRISE

David B. Audretsch

AND

Albert N. Link

OXFORD
UNIVERSITY PRESS

OXFORD
UNIVERSITY PRESS

Oxford University Press, Inc., publishes works that further
Oxford University's objective of excellence
in research, scholarship, and education.

Oxford   New York
Auckland   Cape Town   Dar es Salaam   Hong Kong   Karachi
Kuala Lumpur   Madrid   Melbourne   Mexico City   Nairobi
New Delhi   Shanghai   Taipei   Toronto

With offices in
Argentina   Austria   Brazil   Chile   Czech Republic   France   Greece
Guatemala   Hungary   Italy   Japan   Poland   Portugal   Singapore
South Korea   Switzerland   Thailand   Turkey   Ukraine   Vietnam

Published by Oxford University Press, Inc.
198 Madison Avenue, New York, New York 10016
www.oup.com

Library of Congress Cataloging-in-Publication Data
Audretsch, David B.
Valuing an entrepreneurial enterprise / David B. Audretsch and Albert N. Link.
p. cm.
Includes bibliographical references and index.
ISBN 978-0-19-973037-7 (cloth :alk. paper)
1. New business enterprises—Valuation.   2. Small business—Valuation.
3. Entrepreneurship.   I. Link, Albert N.   II. Title.
HG4028.V3A94 2012
658.15—dc22
2011015274

1 3 5 7 9 8 6 4 2

Printed in the United States of America
on acid-free paper

For Joanne and Carol

CONTENTS

ACKNOWLEDGMENTS

Our sincere thanks to the many individuals who were directly and indirectly involved in the writing and production of this book. We appreciate the confidence of Terry Vaughn, executive editor at Oxford University Press, in our ability to undertake and complete his project, albeit one that is not only provocative but also controversial among valuation practitioners.

Our colleagues, Brittany Atkinson, Samantha Bradley, and Ari Johnson, provided invaluable comments and suggestions on earlier versions of this book. And we especially thank Jamie Link for her insight into the examples used herein.

Of course, we are grateful for the support, encouragement, and patience of our wives Joanne and Carol throughout this process.

ABOUT THE AUTHORS

David B. Audretsch is a distinguished professor and the Ameritech Chair of Economic Development and Director of the Institute for Development Strategies at Indiana University. He received his Ph.D. from the University of Wisconsin. His research has focused on the links between entrepreneurship, government policy, innovation, economic development, and global competitiveness. Audretsch has received support for his research from a broad spectrum of foundations and government agencies, including the Ewing Marion Kauffman Foundation, the Advanced Technology Program of the National Institute of Standards and Technology, the National Academy of Sciences, the U.S. Department of Education, and the National Science Foundation. Notable are his books *Entrepreneurship and Economic Growth* (Oxford University Press, 2006) and *The Entrepreneurial Society* (Oxford University Press, 2007). He is cofounder and coeditor of *Small Business Economics: An Entrepreneurship Journal*. In 2001 he received the International Award for Entrepreneurship and Small Business Research by the Swedish Foundation for Small Business Research.

Albert N. Link is a professor of economics at the University of North Carolina at Greensboro. He received his Ph.D. in economics from Tulane University. His research focuses on innovation policy, academic entrepreneurship, and the economics of R&D. He is the editor-in-chief of the *Journal of Technology Transfer*. Professor Link's most recent books include: *Public Goods, Public Gains: Calculating the Social Benefits of Public R&D* (Oxford University Press, 2011), *Government as Entrepreneur* (Oxford University Press, 2009), and *Cyber Security: Economic Strategies and Public Policy Alternatives* (Edward Elgar, 2008). Much of Professor Link's research has been supported by funding organizations such as the National Science Foundation, the Organization for Economic Co-operation and Development (OECD), the World Bank, the U.S. Department of Energy, and the science and technology ministries in several developed nations. Currently, Professor Link is serving as the vice-chairperson of the Innovation and Competitiveness Policies Committee of the United Nation's Economic Commission for Europe (UNECE).

Introduction

What makes an individual an entrepreneur, and what makes his or her commercial endeavors an entrepreneurial enterprise? These two questions, especially the former, have occupied the minds of many scholars and practitioners for centuries; the answers to each are as varied as those who have given thought to the questions. Envisioning an entrepreneur even occupied the canvas of Maestro Salvador Dali, arguably an entrepreneur in his own right. However, we suspect that few self-proclaimed entrepreneurs would envision themselves as Dali envisioned "The Entrepreneur."

We do not attempt to offer a precise construct or definition of either an entrepreneur or an entrepreneurial enterprise in this book. That is not our purpose in undertaking this project. In fact, others have already trodden that ground.[1] Rather, we offer in this introductory chapter selected, yet relevant, characteristics of an entrepreneur and an entrepreneurial enterprise. The primary emphasis of our effort is on valuation, that is, on how one thinks about or determines the fair market value of an entrepreneurial enterprise.[2] Our emphasis is on closely held entrepreneurial enterprises as opposed to any that are publicly owned.[3]

There are two reasons that we focus on valuation issues and methods that are related to a closely held entrepreneurial enterprise. The first reason is that the number of small, closely held business start-ups, which we refer to broadly as "entrepreneurial enterprises," continues to grow year after year, and new business ventures remain the primary source for employment growth in the United States and most industrialized nations. Second, the topic of the valuation of an entrepreneurial enterprise has for the most part been ignored. The traditional approaches to the valuation of small closely held entrepreneurial enterprises are, in our view, wanting in a number of important respects. Simply, traditional valuation methods are modeled in a manner that is applicable to a going-concern business with a history of sales and revenues. That is not the case for an entrepreneurial enterprise as we define it, and thus the use of traditional valuation methods is questionable.

Through our conceptual discussions and numerical examples, we build on traditional valuation approaches in the chapters that follow, using such approaches much like a straw man to illustrate a more appropriate—and, we suggest, a more accurate—method for dealing with the valuation issues that are relevant to an entrepreneurial enterprise.

To define an entrepreneur, and thus an entrepreneurial enterprise, within the context of valuation, we borrow selectively from others' characterizations of who an entrepreneur is and what he or she does. Motivating the analytical part of this book from this historical and intellectual perspective sets the stage and tone for the remaining chapters.

Our emphasis in this book is on concepts rather than on valuation mechanics; our goal is to provide insight on how one might think about conducting a valuation of an entrepreneurial enterprise. While we do stress the application of widely accepted valuation methods in the following chapters, we are not so much focused on dotting every *i* and crossing every *t*—as one might be in order to meet Generally Accepted Accounting Principles (GAAP) or U.S.

Internal Revenue Service rulings related to valuations—as we are in emphasizing the lack of applicability of these methods per se to the valuation of an entrepreneurial enterprise. Thus, our presentations in the chapters that follow aim more generally to examine the assumptions that underlie each method and how those assumptions depart from the realities of an entrepreneurial enterprise.

The thrust of our message is simple. When valuing an entrepreneurial enterprise—a technology-based entrepreneurial enterprise in particular—the key to approaching the valuation is to focus on and understand the availability of alternative or complementary technologies rather than the existence of substitutable products.[4]

1.1 DEFINING AN ENTREPRENEUR

Before defining an entrepreneur, we turn to the intellectual history of thought about such a person.[5] We first reflect selectively on Joseph Schumpeter's view of an entrepreneur as an innovator, and we consider his thought further in Chapter 2. Schumpeter viewed entrepreneurial activity within the context of a theory of economic development. According to Schumpeter:

> [E]veryone is an entrepreneur only when he actually "carries out new combinations [of resources]," and loses that character as soon as he has built up his business, when he settles down to running it as other people run their businesses.
>
> (1934, p. 78)

Schumpeter goes on to say that implementing new ideas and discovering new combinations of resources define an entrepreneur as a disequilibrating agent of change; the purposeful environment in which this occurs is an entrepreneurial enterprise. Thus, it is clear that the entrepreneur in Schumpeter's domain is the key agent of economic growth and development. Schumpeter (1934, p. 74) was quite emphatic about this role of the entrepreneur when he wrote, "The carrying out of new combinations we call 'enterprise'; the individuals whose function it is to carry them out we call 'entrepreneurs.'"[6]

With this Schumpeterian view of the entrepreneur in mind, we also reflect on the thoughts of Nobel laureate T. W. Schultz (1975). He defined entrepreneurship simply as the ability to deal with disequilibria.[7] Thus, Schultz widened Schumpeter's concept of entrepreneurship to include any economic agent who has this ability. Schultz insisted that the supply of such entrepreneurial talent is a scarce economic resource. This view logically raises the question: if such talent is scarce, where does one acquire the ability to deal with disequilibria?

Fritz Machlup, who reflected on the general writings of earlier scholars and on the implications of Schultz's definition of an entrepreneur, answered this question, at least in part. Machlup argued that formal education, which is largely based on codified knowledge, is not the only source of knowledge upon which an entrepreneur might draw. Rather, knowledge is also gained experientially, and experiential education is often based on tacit knowledge. Individuals can acquire knowledge from their day-to-day experiences, which "will normally induce reflection, interpretation, discoveries, and generalizations" (Machlup 1980, p. 179). Moreover, the cost of acquiring experiential knowledge and knowing that it has in fact been acquired, is related to differential abilities, some of which may be learned but others that are likely instinctive:

> Some alert and quick-minded persons, by keeping their eyes and ears open for new facts and theories, discoveries and opportunities, perceive what normal people of lesser alertness

and perceptiveness would fail to notice. Hence new knowledge is available at little or no cost to those who are on the lookout, full of curiosity, and bright enough not to miss their chances.

(Machlup 1980, p. 179)

We suggest that Machlup's view offers some initial insight to the question about where one acquires the ability to deal with disequilibria. One acquires—likely over time—an ability to deal with disequilibria by continuing to be perceptive, that is, by continuing to be on the lookout, by continuing to be full of curiosity, and by continuing to be bright enough not to miss opportunities.[8]

Here, we view an entrepreneur and his or her enterprise very broadly. An entrepreneur is one who perceives an opportunity and has the ability to act on that opportunity. For the purpose at hand, it does not matter whether the entrepreneur provoked the change that created the opportunity or simply perceived that it existed.[9] Either way, action implies that the entrepreneur had the courage to embrace risk in the face of uncertainty. And thus, an entrepreneurial enterprise, be it physical or virtual, is the manifestation of the entrepreneur's perception and action.[10]

1.2 DEFINING AN ENTREPRENEURIAL ENTERPRISE

Our point of departure from this conceptual entrepreneur and entrepreneurial enterprise to a specific type of real-world business venture is based on our prior experiences and abilities. Our definitions reflect our decades of research in the areas of entrepreneurship, technology, and innovation, as well as our practitioner-related valuation experience. Our emphasis in this book is thus logically on one specific type of entrepreneurial enterprise, namely one that is technology-based.

Although some might say that our focus is overly narrow, we respectfully dismiss that point of view. The valuation principles for an entrepreneurial enterprise that we espouse in this book are indeed widely applicable. We also believe that most entrepreneurial births in the coming decade will have at least some, if not a significant amount of, technological basis.

In the following chapters, we set forth a general method for valuing a technology-based entrepreneurial enterprise. Again, our focus is not just on any technology-based business but rather on one that is a closely held embryonic start-up with no sales history upon which to forecast its future revenues. By definition, there are no other businesses that produce a substitutable or even similar product, or that are even comparable in other dimensions. This is an important point throughout the book.

The extant valuation literature is replete with approaches to valuing a going-concern business—technology based or otherwise—that has a well-documented history of sales or revenues. Such is the state of the art in the practice of valuation regardless of the background of the person conducting it; unfortunately, that state of the art is not applicable—some might say not even remotely applicable—to the current and growing population of technology-based entrepreneurial enterprises in need of a valuation.

Of course, and at the risk of throwing rocks at our own glass houses, many professional and certified valuators and self-identified practitioners have for the most part skirted this important issue by simply assuming the problem away through legerdemain. For example, some are content simply to say that the valuation of an entrepreneurial enterprise is tricky and leave it at that.[11]

Those who have not skirted the issue have approached it incorrectly, we believe. We have often heard from professional and certified valuators, and even more frequently read in treatises and textbooks, that traditional evaluation approaches are directly applicable to any entrepreneurial undertaking. All one must do, such valuation pundits often say, is assume the to-be-valued business's revenue history can be approximated by that of a comparable company, where "comparable" refers to a company selling a substitute product.[12]

If one buys into this argument, the substitute product becomes the yardstick by which to measure the expected future market success, and hence the market value, of the entrepreneurial enterprise. But does such a yardstick even exist? In our opinion, it does not, and those who advocate the view that one does are at best naïve and at worst rather cavalier. More importantly, those who hold such a view are apparently oblivious to the reality that theirs is a view based on internally inconsistent facts. First, as we have previously stated, if the enterprise is truly entrepreneurial, by definition there would be no other comparable company either in terms of selling or developing a substitutable or similar product.

Second, if there were in fact another company that was producing a substitute or similar product, the to-be-valued enterprise in question would by definition not truly be entrepreneurial. Assuming that this to-be-valued enterprise was attempting to enter a market in which there was another similar company, the existing company's revenue history or market penetration might still be irrelevant for a fair market valuation of the entrepreneurial enterprise because the growth path of the existing company occurred in a market environment that lacked competition. Vying for market shares leads to a number of rivalrous behaviors, including advertising, price competition, and quality competition.

And third, even if a historically operating technology-based company could be identified, it would neither be relevant to the current economic environment nor representative of the to-be-valued business because it, unlike the to-be-valued business, has a history of being successful in the marketplace. One does not know and should not assume that the entrepreneurial enterprise will be successful over time.[13]

1.3 MOTIVATING OUR EMPHASIS ON ENTREPRENEURIAL ENTERPRISES

Our approach to valuing a technology-based entrepreneurial enterprise, as alluded to earlier, rests on an understanding of the role of alternative or complementary technologies. In most instances, any innovation that an entrepreneur is trying to develop from a new or burgeoning technology will only penetrate the market once attendant technologies are in place. Thus, forecasting alternative or complementary technologies, and their market impact, is the key to valuing an entrepreneurial enterprise.

The need for a systematic methodology is, we believe, great and growing. Below we offer some generalized statistics that address the breadth of the landscape to which our methodology might apply. These statistics motivate the question: how many new technology-based entrepreneurial ventures are in need of valuation each year?

We attempt to answer this question by considering a number of statistics from a variety of sources. Each of these statistics is likely a point estimate, meaning that each has an equal probability of being too large or too small.[14] However, each statistic comes from well-documented sources, so each likely represents the best available information on the subject.

Our approach to answering the question of how many new technology-based entrepreneurial ventures are in need of valuation each year begins with selected information specific to the United States. However, we will extrapolate our findings to the rest of the world. The U.S. Small Business Administration Office of Advocacy reported that in 2007 there were nearly 670,000 small business births in the country, where "small business" refers to a company with a beginning year employment of less than 500.[15] Of those 670,000 small business births, about 640,000 had a beginning year employment of less than 20.[16]

The number of small business births in the United States has increased steadily for nearly two decades even with the intermittent and expected dips during recessionary times. For example, the Small Business Administration's Office of Advocacy (2010) estimated that U.S. small business births in 2009, near the trough of the current business cycle, were just over 550,000. Even if these burgeoning enterprises are short lived, all are likely to need a valuation at some point in time for seeking venture capital, borrowing funds from third parties, or being sold.[17] But our focus in this book is delimited; we are addressing only technology-based enterprises.

Using 600,000 as a conservative illustrative steady-state number of total new business births per year in the United States, at least 12 percent will be technology based. Reynolds and Curtin (2008, p. 214) estimated from their analysis of the Panel Study of Entrepreneurial Dynamics that, on average, 12 percent of start-ups "initiated patent, copyright, or trademark protection." Thus, we offer here 72,000 (i.e., 12 percent of 600,000) as a lower-bound point estimate of the steady-state number of new technology-based enterprises in the United States that will potentially need to be valued each and every year.

To substantiate the lower-bound nature of this number of 72,000—aside from the conservative base of 600,000 from which it came—note that it does not take into account valuation issues related to spin-off divisions of companies established under the umbrella of the parent company that are pursuing a new technology-based product. To our knowledge, there are no estimates for this umbrella effect, but if the popular press accounts are a barometer, the number of new technology-based enterprises in the United States that will potentially need to be valued each year may be much greater than our conservative estimate of 72,000.

Globally, the annual number of entrepreneurial enterprises in need of a valuation is much larger. Mason, for example, suggested that "with 472 million entrepreneurs worldwide attempting to start 305 million companies, approximately 100 million new businesses (or one third) will open each year around the world" (2010, p. 3). And, if 12 percent of these 100 million new businesses are technology based, the potential applicability of the methodology we offer herein is vast.

1.4 AN OVERVIEW OF THE BOOK

The remainder of the book is outlined as follows. Chapter 2 provides a general discussion of alternative economic frameworks for analyzing innovative activity in general. Alternative approaches to innovation, and their implications for public policy, are compared and contrasted. These approaches include the neoclassical model, the Keynesian model, and the Schumpeterian model. Each model's framework provides a distinct view for understanding and valuing innovative activity. This discourse underscores the topical nature and importance of entrepreneurship, innovation, and the entrepreneurial enterprise. More to the point, our purpose in Chapter 2 is to identify and unravel the disparate views toward innovation that are prevalent within the community of economics and to link them to the various public policy approaches. These disparate schools of thought, or ways of thinking about the economy in general and about the role of entrepreneurship and innovation in particular, not only shape how innovation and entrepreneurial activity is valued, but also the overall policy debate concerning innovation and entrepreneurship. Our analysis of these views sets the stage for how we, as academic economists and experienced valuators, approach the valuation of an entrepreneurial enterprise.

The remaining chapters are applied in their content and their structure. Chapter 3 summarizes several basic valuation tools. These tools include forecasting, calculation of weighted averages, present value and capitalization, and selected dimensions of risk analysis. Each of these tools is fundamental to the implementation of a traditional approach to valuation, and we discuss each of them in general terms as background. Each will specifically be referred to in subsequent chapters both in concept and in terms of illustrative calculations.

Chapter 4 illustrates, through example, income-based and asset-based valuation methods. We refer to these as the traditional approaches to valuation. Each method is based on the financial history of the company as represented by their Income Statement and Balance Sheet, but of course that financial history does not exist in an entrepreneurial enterprise as we have defined one. We describe the general procedures of these methods to establish a benchmark or frame of reference for arguing that they are inappropriate for the valuation of an entrepreneurial enterprise.

In Chapter 5 we illustrate the relevant calculations necessary to implement each of the valuation methods described in Chapter 4 using a simple and hypothetical Income Statement and Balance Sheet for a going concern.

Chapter 6 builds on Chapter 5 by introducing, through a case study, the importance of understanding complementary technology infrastructure in the valuation of a technology-based business. The case study is of a small, family-owned video rental company. While not strictly an entrepreneurial enterprise in our definitional sense, it serves as a stepping stone to the remaining chapters. Specifically, the valuation of the video rental company illustrates the importance of knowing about complementary technology when estimating the expected life of a business.

In Chapter 7 we point out, in piecemeal fashion, how each of the valuation steps for the four valuation methods discussed in Chapters 4 and 5 are inapplicable to an entrepreneurial enterprise.

Chapter 8 is a second case study. It addresses the valuation of an entrepreneurial enterprise for which there are no similar or substitute products. The specific example is a company that is researching the potential use of lighter metal materials in passenger automobiles in order to achieve greater fuel efficiency. However, it is well known that the severity of an accident increases as the weight, and thus the strength, of the automobile decreases. It is unlikely that the automobile industry will use these new materials in automobiles, and it is unlikely that consumers will purchase automobiles made of them, unless there is a compensating factor to offset the increased probability of severe injuries from an accident. The compensating factor rests on a complementary technology that affords the driver and passenger(s) greater safety. Accident-warning and accident-avoiding technologies are being developed, based on sensor technologies, to both warn the driver of an impending accident and to take control of the automobile should the driver not respond. We illustrate how to value a materials-producing company, although it has no current sales or revenues, by focusing on the development of the sensor technology.

Chapter 9 concludes the book with a brief summary statement.

NOTES

1 Hébert and Link (1988, 2009) have provided the definitive historical trace of who the entrepreneur is and what he or she does.

2 Fair market value refers to the price at which tangible property would be exchanged between a willing and fully informed buyer and a willing and fully informed seller, neither of whom is under duress to buy or sell the property.

3 A closely held business is one for which the ownership is held by one or more individuals. There is no publicly traded stock.

4 In economics, a substitute is defined as a good or service purchased and used in place of another good or service. A complement is defined as a good or service purchased and used together with another good or service. Henceforth, we depart from the more traditional terminology in economics of "good or service," and we use the term *product*.

5 Hébert and Link (2009) write that the historical literature in economics offers at least a dozen somewhat overlapping characterizations of who the entrepreneur is and what he or she does. These characterizations of an entrepreneur include: the person who assumes the risk associated with uncertainty, the person who supplies financial capital, an innovator, a decision maker, an industrial leader, a manager or superintendent, an organizer and coordinator of resources, the owner of an enterprise, an employer of factors of production, a contractor, an arbitrageur, and an allocator of resources among alternative uses.

6 According to Hébert and Link (2009), Schumpeter's entrepreneur was the motivating force of economic change. The talented few who carry out innovations by devising new technologies, discovering new products, and developing new markets account for the short and long cycles of economic life. Schumpeter saw economic development as a dynamic process, a disturbance of the status quo. He viewed economic development not as a mere adjunct to the central body of orthodox economic theory, but as the basis for reinterpreting a vital process that had been crowded out of mainstream economic analysis by the static, general equilibrium approach. The entrepreneur is a key figure for Schumpeter because he is, quite simply, the *persona causa* of economic development, and economic development occurs in industrial and commercial life by the carrying out of new combinations in production.

It is accomplished by an entrepreneur who is first and foremost an innovator. Schumpeter described innovation in several ways. Initially he spelled out the kinds of new combinations that underlie economic development. They encompass the following: (1) creation of a new good or new quality of good, (2) creation of a new method of production, (3) the opening of a new market, (4) the capture of a new source of supply, (5) a new organization of industry (e.g., creation or destruction of a monopoly). In Schumpeter's theory, successful innovation requires an act of will, not of intellect. It therefore depends on leadership, not intelligence; it should not be confused with invention. On this last point, Schumpeter (1934, pp. 88–89) was explicit: "To carry any improvement into effect is a task entirely different from the inventing of it, and a task, moreover, requiring entirely different kinds of aptitudes. Although entrepreneurs of course may be inventors just as they may be capitalists, they are inventors not by nature of their function but by coincidence and vice versa. Besides, the innovations which it is the function of entrepreneurs to carry out need not necessarily be any inventions at all." The leadership that constitutes innovation in the Schumpeterian system is disparate, not homogeneous. An aptitude for leadership stems in part from the use of knowledge, and knowledge has aspects of a public good. People of action who perceive and react to knowledge do so in various ways; each internalizes the public good in potentially a different way. The leader distances himself from the manager by virtue of his aptitude. According to Schumpeter (1928, p. 380), different aptitudes for the routine work of "static" management result merely in differential success at what all managers do, whereas different leadership aptitudes mean that "some are able to undertake uncertainties incident to what has not been done before; [indeed] ... to overcome these difficulties incident to change of practice is the function of the entrepreneur." See Hébert and Link (2009) for a more detailed explanation of Schumpeter's views and how they relate to those of his predecessors.

7   Whereas Schumpeter's entrepreneur brought about disequilibrium, Schultz's entrepreneur is an economic agent who has the ability to deal with that disequilibrium. We revisit this point below.

8   While this statement does open the door to a discussion about whether entrepreneurial ability is learned through nature or obtained from nurture, we hereby close it by stating that, as interesting as such a discussion is, it is out of bounds for the purpose of this book.

9   Hébert and Link (2009, p. 105) address this distinction by posing the following question: "Does it matter whether the entrepreneur is the person who provokes change or merely [the person who] adjusts to it? If we rely on the most elemental features of entrepreneurship—perception, courage [to take on risk], and action—the answer is probably not. Entrepreneurial action means creation of opportunity as well as response to existing circumstances."

10 A provocative question from the perspective of intellectual thought about entrepreneurship is: can a business or enterprise be an entrepreneur, or is an enterprise entrepreneurial because it is owned and managed by an entrepreneur(s)? We believe that the answer to both of these question is no, and our reasoning is as follows. Humans rather than institutions make decisions, and entrepreneurial decisions thus characterize an entrepreneurial enterprise. But we do acknowledge that there is another side to the coin. One might argue that an enterprise is simply the aggregation of individual decision makers who have a collective will revealed through some system of rules. Under this scenario, one might make a case for an enterprise as being an entrepreneur.

11 In our opinion, Nollsch (2010) correctly states that "valuation is a tricky subject for early-stage entrepreneurs raising capital. With a limited performance history of the business, how do you accurately determine valuation?" He also states, "The best thing an entrepreneur can do to increase their chances of funding and improve their valuation is to focus on lowering the risk profile [being] executed on the business plan.... Ultimately, valuation for early stage companies is a negotiation exercise and requires a bit of haggling back and forth." We disagree that the best thing an entrepreneur can do is focus on lowering the risk profile of his or her enterprise, and we argue in this book that it is possible—for a technology-based enterprise in particular—to conduct a systematic valuation using traditional valuation tools.

12 We have frequently heard this argument made by professional and certified valuators in many a practitioner-filled seminar room, and almost without thinking, those in attendance simply nod their heads as if saying, "Yes, I agree." No one is to blame, we suggest; rather, we believe that others have not thought through the issue of valuating an entrepreneurial enterprise, or they have thought through the issue but are not of the mindset to integrate the pending influence of complementary technologies into their traditional framework of analysis.

13 Acs and Mueller (2008) present empirical information that suggests that the average effective life of an entrepreneurial start-up is short, perhaps not longer than five years.

14 Regardless of the variance in each datum that follows, the entire body of information emphatically makes the point that the population of technology-based entrepreneurial enterprise in need of valuation is large.

15 There are births and deaths of small businesses every year. In 2009, the turnover rate (i.e., total deaths divided by total births) in the United States was 0.90 (U.S. Small Business Administration 2009). This statistic does not imply that 90% of all small businesses started in 2009 died that same year. Rather, the total number of small firms started in previous years that died in 2009 was 90% of the total of small firms that were started in 2009. Even dying firms

might be in need of a valuation, if for no other reason than to determine a fair market liquidation value.

16 See http://www.sba.gov/advo/research/dyn_us_tot.pdf.

17 Regarding the population of small businesses in the United States, the following statistics emphasize the number of small-sized firms with fewer than 20 employees in operation. In total, 89.4% of the over six million firms in the United States in 2007 had fewer than 20 employees (U. S. Census Bureau 2007). This percentage, based on Census Bureau data for 2007 for a number of sectors includes the following: forestry, fishing, hunting, agriculture support – 93.7%; mining – 81.5%; construction – 91.7%; manufacturing – 74.3%; wholesale trade – 85.7%; retail trade – 90.6%; transportation and warehousing – 87.8%; real estate and rental and leasing – 95.1%; professional, scientific, and technical services – 93.5%; educational services – 77.3%; health care and social assistance – 87.1%; and accommodation and food services – 79.8%.

2

Innovative Activity
Alternative Economic Frameworks and Policy Approaches

The way that someone thinks about the value of entrepreneurship along with the ensuing innovative activity is shaped by the framework or model, be it explicit or implicit, underlying his or her views. This is just as true for professional economists as it is for policymakers and practitioners. If there were only a singular underlying framework or view there would be more of a consensus concerning the role and value of entrepreneurship and innovation, as well as the appropriate public policy stance to encourage both.

However, there is anything but unanimity when it comes to economic thinking about the role—and therefore the economic value—of innovative activity in the economy. This ambiguity is reflected by disparate approaches toward public policy. The lack of convergence toward a singular model or framework for understanding the role of entrepreneurship and innovative activity in the economy has resulted in what must seem like a Tower of Babel in the professional pronouncements of economists and policymakers alike on entrepreneurship and innovation.

Despite the confusion generated by disparate views of how the economy actually works and therefore how entrepreneurship and innovation should be valued—and valuing entrepreneurship and innovation is at the heart of valuing an entrepreneurial enterprise—the importance of the economic doctrines underlying the prevalent frameworks for thinking about the economy should not be underestimated. As John Maynard Keynes once observed:

> The ideas of economists and political philosophers, both when they are right and when they are wrong, are more powerful than is commonly understood. Indeed the world is ruled by little else. Practical men, who believe themselves to be quite exempt from any intellectual influence, are usually the slaves of some defunct economist.
>
> (1935, p. 376)

Our purpose in this chapter is to identify and unravel the disparate views toward innovation prevalent within the economic community and to link them to the various public policy approaches. These various schools of thought, or ways of thinking about the economy in general and the role of entrepreneurship and innovation in particular, not only shape how innovation and entrepreneurial activity are valued, but also the overall policy debate concerning innovation and entrepreneurship. Our unraveling of these views sets the stage for how we, as academic economists and experienced valuators, approach the valuation of an entrepreneurial enterprise.

The remainder of this chapter is divided into six sections. Several main economic doctrines are introduced in Section 2.1 and put into the context of the historical, social, and economic forces that gave birth to their unique approach to understanding and analyzing the economy. In the Section 2.2, the neoclassical model of economics and the role that entrepreneurship and innovation play in that model are explained. The Keynesian framework of economics, along with its views toward innovation and entrepreneurship, follows in Section 2.3. In Section 2.4, the framework of Schumpeterian economics and its central focus on innovation and entrepreneurship, introduced in Chapter 1, is explained further. Section 2.5 compares and contrasts the role of innovation and entrepreneurship, and the public policy response, in each of these economic doctrines. Finally, in Section 2.6, we provide a summary and our conclusions. In particular, this chapter suggests that much of the thinking and confusion concerning the role of innovation and entrepreneurship reflects the instincts and insights of traditional economic frameworks that do not have a central focus on innovation and entrepreneurship.

2.1 DISPARATE SCHOOLS OF ECONOMIC THINKING

There are three main or dominant modes that have shaped thinking about economics and therefore have provided the intellectual underpinning for valuing entrepreneurship and innovation. These economic doctrines are commonly referred to as neoclassical economics, Keynesian economics, and Schumpeterian economics. Each of these views or frameworks provides a coherent, logical, and consistent way of thinking about and analyzing the economy.

These disparate views of economics vary in a number of fundamental ways. First, they differ on what they consider is of primary importance in the economy. Second, they differ on the mechanisms that influence the primary focus. And third, they differ on the appropriate stance and role for public policy. It is important to recognize that these prevailing economics doctrines compete for the attention and allegiance of policymakers, both in the United States as well as elsewhere in the world. It is also important to recognize that the role of entrepreneurship and innovation differ considerably across these main economic frameworks.

One of the reasons such disparate views of the role of entrepreneurship and innovation exist within these three economic frameworks is that they did not emerge in an intellectual vacuum. Rather, they coalesced around a set of political, economic, and social forces within a particular historical context. The *Zeitgeist* of a particular era profoundly shapes the dominant thinking and what ultimately emerges as a fundamental economic doctrine. For example, prior to World War II, the dominant economic doctrine was classical economics, drawing directly on the work and ideas of Adam Smith and David Ricardo. A fundamental feature, even belief, of classical economics was the primacy of unfettered private markets, which allowed for minimalist government intervention.

However, with the onset of the Great Depression in the 1930s, which brought unemployment to one-quarter of the workforce as well as persistently low—even negative—rates of economic growth, the prevalent doctrine of neoclassical economics gave way to a new view of the economy known as Keynesian economics. Following the Great Depression and World War II, Keynesian economics emphasized using federal government spending and other public policies to stimulate demand and manage the business cycle. The extent to which Keynesian economics had emerged as the dominant paradigm in the post-war era was evident in 1971, when President Richard Nixon proclaimed, "We are all Keynesians now."

A historical irony of President Nixon's blanket acknowledgment of the pervasiveness of Keynesian economics was that the theory was on the brink of collapse. Once again, the social, economic, and political landscapes changed. Within months of President Nixon's declaration, severe inflation and simultaneous high unemployment hit the United States. The country was besieged by severe inflation and simultaneous high rates of unemployment, in what famously became referred to as "stagflation." The Keynesian policy prescription—managing aggregate demand or spending in the economy—was only able to mitigate one of the problems while aggravating the other; this became known as a policy tradeoff between inflation and unemployment.

Rather than accept the pessimistic view and policy tradeoff, economists developed a new doctrine, which at the time was known as supply-side economics. This new approach shifted focus from the aggregate demand or spending side of the economy to the economy's ability to supply goods and services—the supply side.

As emphasized in the following sections, neither the neoclassical nor the Keynesian view focuses on the role of entrepreneurship and innovation. However, as the era of globalization emerged in the 1990s and continued into this century, innovation seemed to become more of a central strategy to generate competitiveness in globally linked markets. Certainly the Lisbon European Council of 2000 identified innovation as the key to economic growth and job creation in Europe. The increased attention to the importance of entrepreneurship and innovation led to at least the beginnings of a new economic doctrine that focuses on the centrality of these concepts. While the intellectual underpinnings date back at least to Schumpeter, the focus of the so-called Schumpeterian framework is on the ability of the economy to engage in innovative activity in order to generate economic growth and employment.

2.2 THE NEOCLASSICAL ECONOMIC VIEW

Neoclassical economics has its intellectual roots in Smith's 1776 treatise *An Inquiry into the Nature and Causes of the Wealth of Nations.* The major concern of neoclassical economics is the allocation of resources to maximize, in a static sense, the economic well-being of the population, given the distributions of wealth and income. Thus, neoclassical economics focuses on markets and prices as the mechanisms that allocate scarce resources to produce the goods and services that satisfy (unlimited) consumer wants. In fact, a distinguishing feature of neoclassical economics is the centrality of market-determined price signals.

The market is so central to the neoclassical economic framework because it is the sole institution generating the prices upon which individuals and firms base their decisions. The decision making of firms and individuals is assumed to be rational. Individuals rely on market-generated prices to make their consumption and work decisions, and firms respond through their decisions about what to produce and how to produce it. The assumption of rationality in the neoclassical economic doctrine ensures that decision makers will place primacy on prices in making their decisions. As prices change, so too will their decisions. Thus, according to Laffer (2004, p. 1), inherent in neoclassical economics "is a recognition that people change their behavior when marginal incentives change."

In understanding and analyzing the economy, neoclassical economics prefers the application of abstract mathematical models rather than detailed studies of actual individuals, businesses, industries, regions, or entire national economies. Such abstract neoclassical models almost inevitably revolve around the maximizing behavior of individuals and firms in responding rationally to market-determined price signals. The primacy of market-determined prices in driving the decision making of individuals—both as consumers and as workers—and firms leaves little room for understanding or analyzing decisions about innovative activity, which often involve the creation of markets that do not even exist at that time.

Thus, innovative activity seems to be peripheral in the neo-classical economic framework because it falls outside of existing markets and their prices. Ideas and visions that lie within the dreams and aspirations of men and women are not conducive to static equilibrium models revolving around maximizing behavior of individuals. The assumption of perfect information and knowledge inherent in the neoclassical framework assumes away the most crucial dimensions driving innovative activity.

A key implication of the assumptions underlying the neoclassical economic doctrine is that the essential elements—prices and markets—tend to become obscured across countries. Particularly in the contemporary era of rapidly globalizing economies, where global markets replace regional and national markets, neoclassical economics has the peculiar feature of rendering local or national institutions as irrelevant or at least not particularly important. Thus, neoclassical economists tend to acknowledge few essential institutional differences across national contexts, since the laws of neoclassical economics are considered to apply in the same way to all country contexts at all points of time. That is, time and space do not play a central role in explaining or understanding economic phenomena. Rather, the primacy of prices and markets and their role in shaping the decisions of individuals and firms drive economic phenomena. As Atkinson and Audretsch point out:

> It is for this reason that neoclassical economics largely overlooks factors such as economic history, culture, norms, and institutions, preferring instead to dwell in the more universal world of prices, costs, and mathematical models. It is also for this reason that most neoclassical economists reject the notion of a new

economy emerging in the last decade, because for them, the economy is still based on price signals and supply and demand.

(2010, p. 6)

The economy is working well, and the economic goal is attained when allocative efficiency is realized. This suggests maximum consumer satisfaction, given an endowment of resources, is obtained. The presumed rationality of individual decision making is interpreted as tantamount to the public interest. As Smith instructed, an individual who "intends only his own gain" through rational maximization of utility will inevitably be "led by an invisible hand to promote ... the public interest" (2000, p. 23).

Thus, in the neoclassical economic framework, the focus is on static equilibrium and the use of markets to allocate resources. This leaves little room for the analysis or understanding of entrepreneurship and innovation. According to neoclassical economics, public policy has little role—other than minimizing government-induced distortions in markets—in ensuring that the economy is performing at a high level. There are two main reasons for this minimalist view. The first is that unfettered market forces ensure that the economy tends toward a high-performance equilibrium. As long as there is competition, the forces of supply and demand will generate market prices that will induce consumers and producers to act in ways that move the economy toward equilibrium. Prices of unemployed or underemployed resources, such as labor, will tend to fall, inducing producers to utilize them. One acknowledged role for government policy is to ensure that any artificially created barriers to entry or impediments to equilibrating markets are eliminated or mitigated. So long as there are no impediments or barriers to the process of markets equilibrating, there is no mandate or need for government intervention.

The second reason for limiting government's role is that even when economic performance is not satisfactory, such as times of high unemployment or low growth rates, government intervention is essentially futile. The prevalent view among neoclassical economics is that government policy can do little to influence the supply side of the economy with the exception of minimizing government-induced distortions in markets. In other words, "although economists can tell the government much about how to influence aggregate demand, they can tell it precious little about how to influence aggregate supply. Let no supply-sider tell you differently" (Blinder 1987, p. 107).

What Blinder is referring to with the term *supply-sider* is an offshoot from the neoclassical economic doctrine that differs not in the assumptions, analyses, methods, and focus of the neoclassical economic framework, but rather the main public policy prescriptions. Whereas the mainstream neoclassical economic view demands minimalist government intervention, supply-side economics advocates an active public policy role to minimize it. The thinking is that taxes imposed on individuals and firms distort market-generated incentives to produce. In particular, it is the marginal tax rates on the wealthiest individuals that exert the greatest dampening impact on productivity, because the wealthiest individuals after all are the most productive and contribute the most to the economic growth of the economy.

Thus, the supply-side economics variant of the neoclassical doctrine focuses the lens of analysis on tax rates, particularly those imposed on the wealthiest individuals. As Blinder advocates, "Every tax influences incentives, as supply-siders correctly emphasize.... Unless the market is malfunctioning, such tax-induced redirections of resources reduce economic efficiency. They are therefore to be minimized" (1987, p. 162).

While the primary focus of the neoclassical economic model is on efficiency in a static sense, both in terms of allocative and productive efficiency, there are also strong implications for economic growth. Nobel laureate Robert Solow (1956) offered insight into economic growth using the framework of neoclassical economics. While two factors, labor and physical capital, determine the level of output in an economy, it is investments in the capital which increases economic growth. Thus, the key to increasing economic growth lies in increasing the stock of physical capital, or investments in plant and equipment. The neoclassical model of economic growth thus framed public policy to focus on targets and instruments that would promote investment in physical capital, such as interest rates and tax depreciation rates for investment.

It would not be quite accurate to say that innovation plays no role in the neoclassical growth model. In fact, Solow did point out that what he termed "technological change" made an important contribution to economic growth. However, the contribution of technological change occurs outside of his explicit growth model and was attributed to the residual, or what could not be explained by the model. Innovation was deemed important but essentially exogenous and unexplained, or outside of the realm of understanding provided by the neoclassical growth model. Thus, rather than being deterministic, technological change falls like manna from heaven.

The supply-side economics offshoot of the neoclassical economic doctrine places an emphasis on policies that create incentives for consumers to save rather than consume. Such savings increase the supply of funds available for capital investment, which in turn lowers the price of borrowing, or the interest rate, to make such investments in capital. Supply-side economists, such as Mankiw, who served as the head of the Council of Economic Advisors under President George W. Bush, is quick to link lower taxes to higher rates of growth: "In the long run, lower tax rates expand the supply side of the economy by enhancing the incentives for work, saving, and investment" (2004, p. 2).

Seen through the lens of the supply-side economics branch of the neoclassical doctrine, the focus and debate involves the interest rate and incentives to save rather than spend. Orszag, who served as director of the Office of Management and Budget, articulated the importance of incentives to save:

> The fundamental benefit of higher national savings—achieved by preserving a substantial portion of the projected budget surplus—is that it will expand economic output in the future. Higher national saving leads to higher investment, which means that future workers have more capital with which to work and are more productive as a result.
>
> (2004, p. 2)

The neoclassical framework is in fact the most dominant and prevalent economic view in the United States. Given its widespread acceptance, what is viewed as the economic mainstream has had a profound impact on shaping the public policy debate, both in terms of the issues considered legitimate public policy concerns as well as the appropriate policy responses and interventions. The neoclassical view has provided the intellectual mandate for a laissez-faire approach to the economy, where government intervention is the exception and occurs only as a last resort. The influence of the neoclassical economic framework and its public policy stance has shaped the policy debate not only in the United States but throughout the world. As the *Wall Street Journal* reports: "Since the end of the Cold War, the world's powers have generally agreed on the wisdom of letting market competition—more than government planning—shape economic outcomes" (Browne and Oster 2010).

However, the neoclassical economic framework has little interest in or focus on the role of entrepreneurship and innovation. According to Mandel, who served as the chief economist of *BusinessWeek*:

> Neoclassical economists are capital fundamentalists who believe that savings and investment in physical capital and (sometimes) human capital are the only forces driving growth. They generally ignore or minimize the role of technology.
>
> (2004, p. 1)

In his critique of the neoclassical economic framework, Mandel points out that in Milton Friedman's best-selling 1979 book *Free to Choose*, the term *technology* does not appear a single time in the index. Mandel suggests this is a reliable indicator of the (lack of) priority assigned to technology and innovation, not just by Friedman, but by the entire doctrine of neoclassical economics. After a careful and critical reading, Mandel concludes that:

> For the most part, neoclassical economists remain profoundly ambivalent or even hostile toward most areas of technology.... They grudgingly acknowledge the importance of technological change, but they don't understand it.
>
> (2004, p.1)

2.3 THE KEYNESIAN VIEW

Keynes and his disciples provided an intellectual response to the economic conditions imposed by the Great Depression of the 1930s.

The classical doctrine in economics was that a level of full employment equilibrium would eventually prevail. After the stock market crash of 1929 and the subsequent drop in gross domestic product, combined with unemployment affecting around one-quarter of the work force, Keynes famously responded that "in the long run, we are all dead." Waiting for markets to restore the economy to full employment seemed less and less like a viable policy option.

Rather than focus on individual markets as the key to economic performance, the framework of Keynesian economics instead shifts the lens of analysis to the total amount of spending, or aggregate demand, in the economy. Too little spending results in low levels of output and high rates of unemployment; too much spending results in inflation. With its central focus on the aggregate demand side of the economy, Keynesian economics takes a radically different view of the role of public policy. Public policy should be responsible for managing aggregate demand, principally through fiscal policy and monetary policy. Fiscal policy includes two main instruments, government spending and taxes. By contrast, monetary policy refers to the money supply, which is managed by the Federal Reserve. Thus, the policy prescription for more economic growth is expansionary fiscal and monetary policies.

The economic crisis of 2008 reflected a sharp drop in aggregate demand due to the failure of banks and other financial institutions, which in turn triggered a drastic drop in wealth in the United States. It was not surprising that the Keynesian policy prescription to restore aggregate demand through stimulus policies became the focal point of the public policy debate. The focus of this debate was on the demand side of the economy. The framework of Keynesian economics has virtually nothing to say about the supply side of the economy, or the ability of the economy to produce goods and services.

Krugman, a leading Keynesian economist, emphasizes that influencing the demand side of the economy should be a priority of government policy, not because the demand side is more important than the supply side of the economy, but because "productivity growth is the single most important factor affecting our economic well-being. But it is not a policy issue, because we are not going to do anything about it" (Krugman 1990, p. 18).

Thus, as under the neoclassical economic framework, Keynesian economics is little concerned with entrepreneurship and innovation. The primacy of the demand side of the economy preempts concern with or attention to key economic phenomena such as entrepreneurship and innovation, which ultimately shape the capacity of an economy to grow, provide jobs, and compete in globalized markets.

2.4 SCHUMPETERIAN ECONOMICS

Just as Smith provided the intellectual underpinnings for classical economics (which gave rise to its contemporary offshoot, neoclassical economics) and Keynes provided the intellectual framework for Keynesian economics, no doubt Joseph Schumpeter is the father of innovation economics. In *Capitalism, Socialism and Democracy*, Schumpeter (1942) shifted the lens of analysis away from the neoclassical emphasis on market-generated static equilibrium and also away from the Keynesian focus on aggregate demand. Instead, Schumpeter put the focus squarely on innovation.

Innovation is first and foremost about change. This change can involve products, processes, organizations, or institutions.

Thus, the Schumpeterian analysis is about change. According to Schumpeter:

> The essential point to grasp is that in dealing with capitalism we are dealing with an evolutionary process...the fundamental impulse that sets and keeps the capitalist engine in motion comes from the new consumers' goods, the new methods of production or transportation, the new markets, the new forms of industrial organization that capitalist enterprise creates.
>
> (1942, p. 37)

Schumpeter's focus was on the driving forces underlying the economy and ultimately generating economic performance. Schumpeter looked at economic performance through a dynamic lens and thus was particularly concerned about growth and economic development. Schumpeter, more than any of the great economists before him, viewed innovation as the driving force of progress and development. According to him:

> It is therefore quite wrong...to say...that capitalist enterprise was one, and technological progress a second, distinct factor in the observed development of output; they were essentially one and the same thing or, as we may also put it, the former was the propelling force of the latter.
>
> (1942, p. 110)

However, the innovative activity driving economic progress, according to Schumpeter, was achieved only at a price; perhaps his most poignant and enduring concept is his view of creative destruction. Just as the factory wiped out the blacksmith shop and the car superseded the horse and buggy, Schumpeter argued that incumbents will be displaced by innovating entrepreneurs. According to McCraw:

> Schumpeter's signature legacy is his insight that innovation in the form of creative destruction is the driving force not only of capitalism but of material progress in general. Almost all businesses, no matter how strong they seem to be at a given moment, ultimately fail—and almost always because they failed to innovate.
>
> (2007, p. 495)

As McCraw explains, "The notion of creative destruction expresses two clashing ideas, not surprising for someone whose personal life embodied so many paradoxes" (2007, p. 3). McCraw emphasizes how Schumpeter seemingly shaped the development of a startlingly unique view of economics. Whereas the classical and neoclassical economists viewed the most essential tension in society as that between capital and labor, Schumpeter was prescient in focusing instead on the clash between the entrepreneurs and the incumbents dependent upon the status quo. As McCraw further points out:

> [Schumpeter] knew that creative destruction fosters economic growth but also that it undercuts cherished human values. He saw that poverty brings misery but also that prosperity cannot assure peace of mind.
>
> (2007, p. 6)

Not only did Schumpeter identify a new economic force—creative destruction—that was pivotal for the functioning of capitalism and consequently economic development, but he also identified the mechanism upon which creative destruction rested, namely the entrepreneur. Schumpeter's entrepreneur served as an agent of change in the economic system; the entrepreneur was the driving force of innovation upon which economic development, growth, and progress rested. Schumpeter argued that what made the entrepreneur different from other agents in the economy was willingness to pursue innovative activity:

> The function of entrepreneurs is to reform or revolutionize the pattern of production by exploiting an invention, or more generally, an untried technological possibility for producing a new commodity or producing an old one in a new way.... To undertake such new things is difficult and constitutes a distinct economic function, first because they lie outside of the routine tasks which everybody understands, and secondly, because the environment resists in many ways.
>
> (1942, p. 13)

Without the entrepreneur, new ideas would not be pursued and implemented. The status quo would tend to be preserved at an opportunity cost of foregone innovative activity, growth, and economic development.

Schumpeter was consistent throughout his life's works about the source of economic growth, creative destruction, which entrepreneurs fueled. Where he was less consistent, generating considerable ambiguity and contention, was about the organizational form and industry structure most conducive to entrepreneurs and innovative activity.

In his 1911 treatise, later translated as the *Theory of Economic Development*, Schumpeter proposed a theory of creative destruction, in which he was unambiguous about the organizational structure most conducive to entrepreneurs: new firms infused with entrepreneurial spirit would displace the tired old incumbents, ultimately leading to vigorous innovative activity which in turn would generate a higher degree of economic growth. As Scherer pointed out:

> Schumpeter insisted that innovations typically originated in new, characteristically small, firms commencing operation outside the 'circular flow' of existing production activities. To be sure, the small innovating firms that succeeded would grow large, and their leaders would amass great fortunes. They started, however, as outsiders.
>
> (1992, p. 1417)

Schumpeter's thinking about the innovative advantage of small firms began to change by the time he published *Business Cycles* in 1939. Rather, he began to recognize that the link between entrepreneurship and the size and age of organizations was more nuanced than he had characterized it in his earlier 1911 book. According to Schumpeter:[1]

> It is, of course, true that mere size is not necessarily an advantage and may well be a disadvantage. Judgment must turn on the merits of each case. But statistical evidence to the effect that smaller concerns often do better than the giants should not be uncritically accepted. The smaller concerns may now often be in the position of the new, and the giants in the position of the old firms in our model. It is held...that the big concerns...implied technological and organizational improvement when they were founded. It is not held that they retrained

their advantages until the present day. Our theory would in fact lead us to expect the contrary.

(1939, p. 4040)

In *Capitalism, Socialism and Democracy*, Schumpeter had rescinded his earlier view about the innovative efficiency of the small enterprise. He concluded that, due to scale economies in the production of new economic knowledge, not only would large corporations have the innovative advantage over small and new enterprises, but ultimately the economic landscape would consist only of giant corporations: "Innovation itself is being reduced to routine. Technological progress is increasingly becoming the business of teams of trained specialists who turn out what is required and make it work in predictable ways" (1942, p. 132).

This is not to say that Schumpeter changed his view about the underlying motivation for innovation:

> Spectacular prizes much greater than would have been necessary to call forth the particular effort are thrown to a small minority of winners, thus propelling much more efficaciously than a more equal and more "just" distribution would, the activity of that large majority of businessmen who receive in return very modest compensation or nothing or less than nothing, and yet do their utmost because they have the big prize before their eyes and overrate their chances of doing equally well.
>
> (1950, pp. 73–74)

Rather, what had changed was the organizational structure best able to spark and harness entrepreneurial forces. In his earlier years, and certainly in his 1911 book, Schumpeter considered the small enterprise most conducive to the entrepreneurial spirit. But by the time he wrote *Capitalism, Socialism and Democracy*, he had concluded that while entrepreneurship was needed to generate the process of creative destruction, this could best be financed, organized, and harnessed within the organizational structure of the large corporation.

Thus, what changed in *Capitalism, Socialism and Democracy* was that Schumpeter rejected his own earlier (1911) conclusion that the organizational form most favorable to the entrepreneur was the small business. Instead, by 1942, not only was the large corporation thought to have superior productive efficiency, but Schumpeter also believed it to be the engine of technological change and innovative activity:

> What we have got to accept is that [the large-scale establishment or unit of control] has come to be the most powerful engine of…progress and in particular of the long-run expansion of output not only in spite of, but to a considerable extent through, this strategy which looks so restrictive.
>
> (1942, p. 106)

This was not only a reversal of Schumpeter's own earlier thinking but also a challenge to the prevalent view in economics. According to Scherer:

> Previously it was suggested that monopolists, sheltered from the stiff gale of competition, might be sluggish about developing and introducing technological innovations, which increase productivity (reducing costs) or enhance product quality. Yet, some economists, led by the late Professor Joseph A. Schumpeter, have argued exactly the opposite; firms need protection from competition before they will bear the risks and costs of invention and innovation, and that a monopoly affords an ideal platform for

shooting at the rapidly and jerkily moving targets of new technology. If this is true, then progress will be more rapid under monopoly than under competition.

(1970, pp. 20–21)

The implication of the emerging dominance of the large corporation and competitive unsustainability of the small business, and ultimately capitalism, was clear to Schumpeter: "In this respect, perfect competition is not only impossible but inferior, and has no title to being set up as a model of ideal efficiency" (1942, p. 106).

What exactly had replaced the entrepreneur-driven capitalist economy was a point of contention. Schumpeter was more pessimistic in his 1942 book about socialism replacing capitalism. He gloomily concluded that

since capitalist enterprise, by its very achievements, tends to atomize progress, we conclude that it tends to make itself superfluous—to break to pieces under the pressure of its own success. The perfectly bureaucratic giant industrial unit not only ousts the small- or medium-sized firm and "expropriates" its owners, but in the end it also ousts the entrepreneur and expropriates the bourgeoisie as a class which in the process stands to lose not only in its income but also, what is infinitely more important, its function.

(1942, p. 134)

The dominance of large, entrenched corporations fueled by a seemingly inevitable process of industrial concentration triggering an increased degree of market power and therefore requiring a countervailing public policy, as foreseen by Schumpeter, has not materialized. As Scherer points out in his assessment of *Capitalism, Socialism and Democracy*:[2]

> The book is best known for arguing that by virtue of its success in cranking out goods and services, capitalism would under-mine its own social, organizational, and moral foundations, setting the stage for the ascendance of socialism. Today, as the tumultuous changes in Eastern Europe unfold, that warning appears wildly off the mark.
>
> (1992, p. 1416)

In fact, in what must be one of the greater ironies of history, the mature capitalist countries of the West have not been going through a process of concentration and centralization, as Schumpeter predicted in his later years,[3] but rather a process of deconcentration and decentralization. For example, between 1958 and 1979, the share of sales in the United States accounted for by small firms (with fewer than 500 employees) fell from 52 percent to just 29 percent.[4] Similarly, between 1947 and 1980, real gross national product per firm rose by nearly two-thirds, from $150,000 to $250,000. Curiously, however, within the following six years it dropped sharply by 14 percent, to $210,000. And the amount of employment accounted for by the *Fortune* 500 rose from 8 million (34 percent of total employment) in 1954 to 16 million (58 percent of total employment) by 1979. However, employment accounted for by the *Fortune* 500 proceeded to fall to 11.9 million (40 percent of total employment) by 1991 (Case 1992).

Contrary to Schumpeter's conclusions in his later writing, systematic empirical evidence has found that small and entrepreneurial start-up firms make an important contribution to innovative activity (Audretsch 1995). The reconciliation of the 1942 Schumpeterian position with this empirical evidence lies in the notion of the knowledge filter along with the knowledge spill-over theory of entrepreneurship (Audretsch and Keilbach 2007; Audretsch, Keilbach, and Lehmann 2006). The knowledge filter prevents or impedes knowledge accruing from investments made by incumbent firms and other organizations from actually being implemented and commercialized by that incumbent firm.

An example of the knowledge filter was provided by U.S. Senator Birch Bayh:

> A wealth of scientific talent at American colleges and universities—talent responsible for the development of numer-ous innovative scientific breakthroughs each year—is going to waste as a result of bureaucratic red tape and illogical govern-ment regulations.
>
> (2004, p. 16)

Senator Bayh was pointing to government-imposed restrictions on how intellectual property generated by federally funded scientific research at universities could be used for commercial activities that would ultimately result in innovations. The knowledge filter is a barrier between investments in new ideas—generated by sci-entific research, in the context Senator Bayh was describing—on the one hand and commercialization—which ultimately leads to innovative activity—on the other. The knowledge filter impedes the spillover of knowledge and ideas, thus preventing ideas from becoming innovations in the market. Senator Bayh suggested that, unless the knowledge filter can be penetrated, it is difficult to jus-tify expensive investments in research and development:

> What sense does it make to spend billions of dollars each year on government-supported research and then prevent new

developments from benefitting the American people because of dumb bureaucratic red tape?

(2004, p. 16)

That is, because of the knowledge filter, the billions of dollars poured into investments in research, science, and education do not automatically result in inventions, innovations, or new and better products.

The knowledge filter impedes knowledge spillovers and commercialization based on investments in research at universities and scientific institutions. But universities and other public institutions are not the only places where the knowledge filter blocks investments in ideas and knowledge from becoming commercialized. The knowledge filter is at least as pervasive in the private sector as well.

For example, in Mannheim (in the state of Baden-Wuerttemberg in Germany), five young engineers at IBM—Dietmar Hopp, Hans-Werner Hector, Hasso Plattner, Klaus Tschira, and Claus Wellenreuther—developed an idea for new business software. This idea was the result of costly investment not just by IBM but also by the greater society, in terms of the education the young employees had received in Germany. When they broached the new idea with their boss and their boss's boss, however, they were turned down on the grounds that there did not appear to be a sufficient market for the new software.

The young men were so passionate about and convinced of the importance of their new idea that they tried to obtain funding to start their own company. After the three main banks in Germany— the Dresdner Bank, Deutsche Bank, and Commerzbank—turned them down, they managed to obtain start-up finance through a family connection at a local regional bank near Heidelberg, enabling them to start SAP. By 2009, the business software giant had grown to 47,578 employees in over 50 countries.

How could the decision makers at IBM have been wrong about the value of the innovations proposed by the five young engineers? The knowledge filter. New ideas, which are always the basis for innovative activity, are inherently uncertain. No one can know what outcome or value will be generated from pursuing and implementing new ideas. If this were not the case, the ideas would not really be new.

New ideas also tend to be asymmetric in that the valuation of the new idea by one person is not the same as by other people, even within the same group or organization. This was clearly the case in the example of the new idea generated by the five young engineers at IBM. They obviously placed a high value on their idea, while the parent organization, which had invested a lot of money to develop new ideas, did not.

In addition, the cost of transacting the knowledge of why a new idea is perceived to be valuable is quite high. This is because most innovations are based on tacit knowledge, especially during the earlier stages of their development. The cost of transacting facts or information is almost zero. For example, facts such as the capital of Japan or the temperature in Geneva, Switzerland, can be transacted at virtually no cost. But transacting the beliefs underlying the valuation of a new idea that could potentially lead to innovative activity is complicated and expensive.

The high cost of transacting asymmetric knowledge and beliefs is illustrated by an incident at the Xerox Corporation during the 1970s. Xerox had made substantial investments in research and development of computer technology at its main research facility, Xerox Parc, where many of the main breakthroughs for the personal computer were made. For example, the keyboard, mouse, and screen were all developed at Xerox Parc. However, the company did not pursue commercial development of these products, based on the decision that there was no potential value associated with these inventions. When Steve Jobs saw these inventions, however, he thought they could have enormous value. These inventions, generated by expensive investments made at Xerox, were the basis for Jobs' new company, Apple, and its first product, the Macintosh.

Due to inherent uncertainty, asymmetries, and high transaction costs, it is inevitable that new ideas—whether they are generated by private companies or at universities—will get lost in the knowledge filter. However, as the examples of SAP and Apple suggest, entrepreneurship is an important mechanism that transforms those ideas that might otherwise never get used into innovative activity.

As a result of the knowledge filter, the inability of incumbent firms and organizations to completely commercialize all of the knowledge they create generates opportunities for entrepreneurs to do so by starting a new firm. Thus, entrepreneurship provides a conduit for the spillover of knowledge from the firm and transfers it to a new firm that actually innovates on the basis of that knowledge.

It may be that Schumpeter, in his later years and certainly when he wrote *Capitalism, Socialism and Democracy*, underestimated the key role of entrepreneurship as a conduit for the spillover of knowledge from the organization investing in and creating that knowledge to the new organization actually making the innovations. Certainly the emergence of the entrepreneurial start-up firm as an important source of innovative activity has not escaped the notice of the popular press. *The Economist* reported:

> Despite ever-larger and noisier mergers, the biggest change coming over the world of business is that firms are getting

smaller. The trend of a century is being reversed. Until the mid-1970s, the size of firms everywhere grew; the number of self-employed fell. Ford and General Motors replaced the carriage-maker's atelier; McDonald's, Safeway and W.H. Smith supplanted the corner shop. No longer. Now it is the big firms that are shrinking and the small ones that are on the rise. The trend is unmistakable—and businessmen and policy-makers will ignore it at their peril.

(1989, pp. 173–174)

As Scherer concluded, "Theory and empirical evidence suggest that *Capitalism, Socialism and Democracy* provided faulty guidance concerning the industrial structures most conducive to technological innovation" (1992, p. 1425). "Half a century after the publication of *Capitalism, Socialism and Democracy*, Schumpeter's vision of the industrial structure most conducive to technological progress and hence to economic growth remains both relevant and controversial. The book's publication stimulated a growing stream of theoretical and empirical research. Most of that research supports a conclusion that Schumpeter overstated the advantages of large, monopolistic corporations as engines of technological change" (Scherer 1992, p. 1430).

Whether Schumpeter was more correct about the organizational form most favorable to entrepreneurship and innovation in his earlier or later writings is, of course, very important. However, the point to be emphasized here is that, more than in either of the two other major economic doctrines, Schumpeterian economics asks the relevant questions that focus on innovation and entrepreneurship. The very question posed by Schumpeter, relating organizational type to innovative activity, is not even on the radar screen in the frameworks of neoclassical and Keynesian economics.

2.5 PUBLIC POLICY TOWARD INNOVATION AND ENTREPRENEURSHIP

The public policy stance toward innovation and entrepreneurship differs considerably across the three main economic doctrines. Within neoclassical economics, the role and impact of innovation are hardly noticeable. The focus of neoclassical economics is on efficiency, both in terms of production and allocation of resources for satisfying consumer demands. Neoclassical growth theory has focused predominantly on the role of investment in physical capital as the driver of economic growth. In the neoclassical model, technological change is viewed as being exogenous to what influences economic growth. The main policy instruments are (lower) taxes, such as research and development (R&D) tax credits, which are perceived to alter the incentives to invest in innovative activities. Similarly, entrepreneurship is viewed as a response to incentives. As long as there are no tax or related distortions, market forces will deliver the appropriate supply of entrepreneurship. Instead, the focus of neoclassical economics and its directives guiding public policy is on the efficacy of markets. Neoclassical economics has a market orientation, not an innovation or entrepreneurship orientation.

The focus of Keynesian economics is on restoring economic output to levels compatible with full employment. The main policy target is the (aggregate) demand side of the economy. The main policy instruments are fiscal and monetary policy. The policy focus on aggregate demand assumes that supply will respond to demand. Thus, there is little attention paid to the role or impact of innovation.

By contrast, innovation and entrepreneurship are the primary focal points in Schumpeterian economics. Innovative activity is the key to economic growth, and entrepreneurship is a fundamental behavior upon which innovation is based. Neoclassical economics considers market entry an important economic phenomenon because of its equilibrating impact. Supply will be increased. Entry is about business as usual, only there is more of it. However, viewed through the Schumpeterian lens, entry is important for exactly the opposite reason. It serves to disequilibrate markets through the process of creative destruction. Entry is about change; the entrepreneur who is behind the entry serves as the key agent of change.

The role for public policy in Schumpeterian economics is to facilitate investment in knowledge-creating activities, such as research and education, and to encourage agents of change, or entrepreneurs, to innovate. This leads to a markedly different set of policy targets and instruments than those of neoclassical and Keynesian economics. Policy targets include universities, scientists, schools, and research institutions, as well as nascent entrepreneurs. Policy instruments include funding for research and science, but also funding to start new businesses and become an entrepreneur. Examples of such policy instruments include the Small Business Innovation Research (SBIR) program in the United States (Link and Scott 2010), as well as a myriad of incubators, science parks, and technology transfer programs at universities.

2.6 MAKING SENSE OF IT ALL

In reviewing the relevancy of Schumpeterian economics to the contemporary economic scene, McCraw (2007) suggests the existence of a paradox. On the one hand, he points out that interest in the fundamental subjects of Schumpeter's work—innovation, entrepreneurship, and creative destruction—has never been greater.

He provides vivid examples of how entrepreneurship and innovation have riveted the policy community and the general public across the globe. However, the public policy debate remains, not surprisingly, guided and framed by the neoclassical and Keynesian economic doctrines.

For example, the recent public policy debate about the appropriate response to the financial and economic crises has almost exclusively reflected Keynesian thinking, advocating a very large stimulus policy instead of reduced government spending and lower taxes favored by a neoclassical approach. Noticeably absent has been the Schumpeterian view, which would place the policy priority on innovation and entrepreneurship.

As McCraw (2007) emphasizes, contemporary economics gives scant notice to the work of Schumpeter. As Baumol pointed out, "The theoretical firm is entrepreneurless—the Prince of Denmark has been expunged from the discussion of *Hamlet*" (1968). According to Baumol:

> There is one residual and rather curious role left to the entrepreneur in the neoclassical model. He is the invisible and non-replicable input that accounts for the U-shaped cost curve of a firm whose production function is linear and homogeneous.
>
> (1968)

Public policy reflecting Schumpeterian economics is most relevant in responding to the challenges of globalization. The role of public policy in Schumpeterian economics generally reflects the importance of entrepreneurial start-ups in generating innovation, economic growth, and competitiveness in globally linked markets. For example, Romano Prodi, former president of the European

Commission, proclaimed that the promotion of entrepreneurship was a central cornerstone of European economic growth policy:

> Our lacunae in the field of entrepreneurship needs to be taken seriously because there is mounting evidence that the key to economic growth and productivity improvements lies in the entrepreneurial capacity of an economy.
>
> (2002, p. 1)

With the 2000 Lisbon Proclamation, the European Council made a commitment to becoming not only the leader in knowledge per se, but also the global entrepreneurial leader in order to ensure prosperity throughout the continent.

Europe was not alone in focusing on entrepreneurship as key to generating economic growth. From the other side of the Atlantic, Mowery observes:

> During the 1990s, the era of the "New Economy," numerous observers (including some who less than 10 years earlier had written off the U.S. economy as doomed to economic decline in the face of competition from such economic powerhouses as Japan) hailed the resurgent economy in the United States as an illustration of the power of high-technology entrepreneurship. The new firms that a decade earlier had been criticized by such authorities as the MIT Commission on Industrial Productivity (Dertouzes et al. 1989) for their failure to sustain competition against large non-U.S. firms were seen as important sources of economic dynamism and employment growth. Indeed, the transformation in U.S. economic performance between the 1980s and 1990s is only slightly less remarkable than the failure

of most experts in academia, government, and industry, to predict it.

(2005, p. 1)

Similarly, Bresnahan and Gambardella point out:

Clusters of high-tech industry, such as Silicon Valley, have received a great deal of attention from scholars and in the public policy arena. National economic growth can be fueled by the development of such clusters. In the United States the long boom of the 1980s and 1990s was largely driven by growth in the information technology industries in a few regional clusters. Innovation and entrepreneurship can be supported by a number of mechanisms operating within a cluster, such as easy access to capital, knowledge about technology and markets, and collaborators.

(2004, p. 1)

And Wallsten observes that

policy makers around the world are anxious to find tools that will help their regions emulate the success of Silicon Valley and create new centers of innovation and high technology.

(2004, p. 229)

In the United States, the dominance of neoclassical and Keynesian economics has clearly shaped the public policy debate about how to move the country forward. On the one hand, the public policy community is aware of the key role played by innovation and entrepreneurship in the era of globalization. Both major political parties claim that they are advocates of innovation and entrepreneurship. For example, George W. Bush suggested:

> Seventy percent of the new jobs in America are created by small businesses. I understand that. And I have promoted during the course of the last four years one of the most aggressive, pre-entrepreneur, small business policies....And so in a new term, we will make sure the tax relief continues to be robust for our small businesses. We'll push legal reform and regulatory reform because I understand the engine of growth is through the small business sector.[5]

Even though the roles and impact of entrepreneurship and small businesses can be understood only through the lens provided by Schumpeterian economics, President Bush was resorting to the policy instruments consistent with neoclassical economics.

On the other hand, the awkwardness of linking the dynamic performance of entrepreneurship and innovation through neoclassical economics' static lens was also apparent in President Obama's attempt to reconcile the success of Apple CEO and entrepreneur Steve Jobs to the public policy priority of creating jobs and sustaining the middle class.

A major reason the valuation of innovation and entrepreneurial activity is shrouded in mystery is that the entrenched economic thinking in the United States reflects the two major doctrines—neoclassical economics and Keynesian economics—that give these forces short shrift. By contrast, the basis for understanding and analyzing the impact and role of innovation and entrepreneurship has its roots in the least visible of the triad of economic doctrines—Schumpeterian economics.

NOTES

1   Quoted from Scherer 1992, p. 1417.

2   In fact, Schumpeter himself backed down from making any specific predictions about the inevitable demise of capitalism and emergence of socialism. In his presidential address at the annual meeting of the American Economic Association, Schumpeter (1950, p. 447) cautioned, "I do not 'prophesy' or predict it... (F)actors external to the chosen range of observation may intervene to prevent... consummation." (Quoted from Scherer 1992).

3   For a careful analysis of Schumpeter's prediction that capitalism could not survive, see Scherer 1992.

4   Quoted from *BusinessWeek*; 11/1/93 Bonus Issue, Issue 3344, 10–18.

5   Transcript of President Bush's News Conference, *New York Times*, November 4, 2004, http://www.nytimes.com/2004/11/04/politics/04BUSHTRANS.html?pagewanted=6.

Valuation Methods
Tools of the Trade

Several valuation tools are summarized in this chapter.[1] Certainly, one familiar with valuation methods will have used these tools many times, but these tools and the related discussions ground the examples used in this book. Here we discuss these basic tools at a conceptual level, but we illustrate the use of these tools within the context of implementing alternative valuation methods in Chapter 4. We also refer explicitly to these tools in the valuation examples in each of the subsequent chapters.[2]

The remainder of this chapter is divided into five sections. Forecasting is discussed and illustrated in Section 3.1 followed by weighted averages in Section 3.2. Present value and capitalization are discussed in Section 3.3 and risk analysis in Section 3.4. A brief summary statement concludes the chapter in Section 3.5.

3.1 FORECASTING

Within a valuation context, forecasting is a statistical tool for approximating the value of future business activities, such as sales or revenues. Generally, such future events are estimated on the basis of past events. This obviously invokes two questions. First, is the past a good predictor for the future? Simply, the answer is yes if the economic environment of the past can reasonably be expected to exist in the future, and the answer is no if it cannot. The second question relates to one of the motivations for writing this book. How does one forecast future events for an entrepreneurial enterprise if there are no past events to rely on?

It is intuitive that accurate forecasts are important to a business owner and potential seller, as well as to a potential buyer. Based on precise forecasts the owner can more efficiently and effectively allocate existing resources (whether or not the enterprise is for sale), and the potential buyer can more efficiently and effectively plan for future resource needs should the enterprise be purchased.

By our definition of an entrepreneurial enterprise, forecasting is a moot tool with respect to future sales or revenues because there is no sales or revenue history on which to base a forecast and there are no substitutable or similar products to use as proxies. However, forecasting might still be a useful valuation tool for an entrepreneur to use to estimate the future time path of alternative or complementary technologies.

Implementing a forecasting model is relatively easy because the statistical tools that are needed are part of most computer spreadsheet or statistical software packages. However, implementing a forecasting model *correctly* is a different story, regardless of the spreadsheet or statistical software package at hand.

Assume for illustrative purposes that annual data are available on some business-related variable Y. We represent these data as Y_1, $Y_2, \ldots Y_p$ where the subscript 1 refers to the first year of historical data, the subscript 2 to the second and more recent year of historical data, and the subscript p to the current or present year of data.[3]

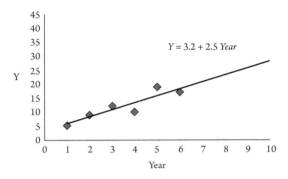

Figure 3.1 Trend Line Forecast

If one were to plot these annual data on a graph on which the variable Y is measured on the vertical axis and years on the horizontal axis, the plot might look like that in Figure 3.1 (p = 6 is the sixth year of data or the current year of data).

A trend line can be constructed to fit to these six data points—more accurately, a spreadsheet or statistical package will fit a trend line to them. The trend line will look like the solid line in the figure relevant to the six data points for years 1, 2, 3, 4, 5, and 6, where year 6 is the current year. In Figure 3.1, three of the six known data points lie above the fitted trend line and three lie below it, some being farther (measured vertically) above or below than others. A trend line is the best linear representation of the six known data points; below, we discuss the criterion that makes this so.

A linear extrapolation of this trend line could be used to calculate a forecast for Y for each of the years 7, 8, 9, and 10, where year 7 is one year into the future, and so on.[4] Of course, one assumption that underlies any forecasted value of Y is that the past events that brought about or influenced the values of Y_1 through Y_6 are accurate predictors of future events that will bring about or influence future values of Y. Stated differently, the values of Y_7 through Y_{10} are based on the assumption that the events in years 1 through 6 will exist in years 7 through 10, and that the events in years 1 through 6 will influence the values of Y in years 7 through 10 to the same extent that they influenced the values of Y in years 1 though 6.

A second assumption is that the estimated trend line—$Y = 3.2 + 2.5(Year)$ as so labeled in Figure 3.1—is in fact the line that best fits the given data. Raising this issue does not suggest that the spreadsheet or statistical software miscalculated the trend line under a set of traditional criteria. Rather, this statement is simply a word of caution that whenever one forecasts with time series data, there are statistical issues that must be considered to ensure that the calculated intercept term—which equals 3.2—and the calculated slope term—which equals 2.5—are, to use a statistical term, *unbiased*.[5]

Assuming that the estimated trend line in Figure 3.1 is the best linear representation of the data for Y_1 through Y_6, future values of Y can be estimated using the equation for the trend line shown in Figure 3.1. These calculations are shown in Table 3.1 for years 7 through 10.

Table 3.1 FORECASTED VALUES OF Y FROM $Y = 3.2 + 2.5\ (Year)$

Value of Year	Forecasted Value of Y
7	$Y = 3.2 + (2.5 \times 7) = 20.7$
8	$Y = 3.2 + (2.5 \times 8) = 23.2$
9	$Y = 3.2 + (2.5 \times 9) = 25.7$
10	$Y = 3.2 + (2.5 \times 10) = 28.2$

Note: By calculation, the forecasted values of Y will lie on the extrapolated portion of the trend line calculated from Y_1 through Y_6.

3.2 WEIGHTED AVERAGES

Common averages are the mean, median (the value in the middle of a set of data), and mode (the most frequently observed value within a set of data). Many, if not most, individuals think of an average value and a mean value as referring to the same calculation; the mean is an average but it is not the only average that can be calculated from a given set of data.

The calculation of a mean value is simple: add up the numerical data and divide by the number of observations. In such a calculation, each value in the set of data is treated equally, meaning that each value has an implicit weight of 1.

Weighted averages are often used in place of a trend line to forecast a value when one wants to assume that certain historical values are more likely to influence future events than are other historical values.[6] Depending on how many historical values are available, or how many historical values are actually relevant for the forecast, alternative weighting schemes might be applicable. Determining the weights to use in the calculation of a weighted average is subjective, but there are some conventions. Calculating the associated weighted values and the weighted average is simple mathematics.

Consider the data for Y used in Figure 3.1 and shown again in Table 3.2. At the current period of time, $Y_6 = 17$. Perhaps Y_6 is a reasonable predictor of Y_7 through Y_{10}. However, there are historical data that might also be relevant. One might assume that future values of Y can simply be estimated as the mean of all available past values of Y, and that mean value is 12.[7] Alternatively, Y_5 may be relevant as a predictor of Y_7 through Y_{10}, but perhaps not as relevant as Y_6 in estimating a future value of Y; Y_4 may be relevant as a predictor of Y_7 through Y_{10}, but not as relevant of a predictor as Y_5 or Y_6, and so on.

If the simple mean value of Y from Y_1 though Y_6 is used to estimate future values of Y, then the implicit assumption is that the past events associated with differences in Y_1 through Y_6 will not exist in the future. The events that will exist in the future are such that they will bring about a future value of Y that equals 12, and that numerical value will not change regardless of what future year is used for a forecast.

Or, one might assume that Y_6 is the best predictor of future values of Y but not the only predictor. Y_5 might be a good predictor, but not quite as good as Y_6; Y_4 might be a good predictor, but not quite as good as Y_5; and so forth. That is, one might assume a weighting

Table 3.2 ILLUSTRATION OF THE CALCULATION
OF A WEIGHTED AVERAGE

Y	Value of Y	Weight	Weighted Value of Y
Y_1	5	1	5
Y_2	9	2	18
Y_3	12	3	36
Y_4	10	4	40
Y_5	19	5	95
Y_6	17	6	102
		21	296
			Weighted average: $296/21 = 14.1$

Note: The weighted value of Y is the product of the value of Y and the weight.

scheme of 6–5–4–3–2–1. With this weighting scheme, the weighted average of the six values of Y is 14.1 as shown in Table 3.2.[8]

Of course, the weighting scheme selected for the calculation of a weighted average is an informed choice. It is certainly not always the case that all of the available historical data are appropriate for calculating a weighted average that will be used to proxy future events. Circumstances vary.

With reference to Table 3.2, a valuator might believe that only the values for Y_4, Y_5, and Y_6 are relevant predictors of future events; the valuator might weight each value using a 1–1–1 weighting scheme (i.e., the valuator might calculate the mean value of the three data points), or the valuator might use a 3–2–1 weighting scheme if it is believed that Y_6 is a better predictor than Y_5, and so forth. However, all three values have relevance in the forecast.

3.3 PRESENT VALUE AND CAPITALIZATION

The economic concept of present value is perhaps the most important concept that is relevant to a valuation, and thus its calculation is likely the most important tool used in a valuation context. Present value (PV) is the value at the present time of all future values of a variable denominated in dollars ($), taking into account that there are alternative uses for that money. That is, PV is the sum of all future values of an investment variable, $X, taking into account that there are alternative uses of money.

More specifically, let $X be the value of an investment expected to exist one year in the future.[9] Let PV represent the present value of $X, and let r represent the alternative use of money, or the rate of return or rate of interest that one can reasonably expect to earn over the one-year period on an investment that is of comparable risk to the investment expected to produce $X in one year. Then, the present value of $X is represented as:

$$PV = \$X / (1+r)^1 \tag{3.1}$$

where r is also referred to as the discount rate.

The logic underlying equation (3.1) is that a present value amount of money, PV, can be invested for one year at rate r to earn $X by the end of that year. At the end of that one-year period one will have the amount originally invested, PV, plus the interest earned on that investment amount, $(r \times PV)$. More specifically, multiplying both sides of equation (3.1) by $(1 + r)^1$ results in:

$$PV \times (1+r)^1 = \$X, \text{ or } PV + (r \times PV) = \$X \tag{3.2}$$

The amount $X is thus the value of an investment of PV dollars now to earn interest over one year at the rate r. Or, an investment of PV now to earn interest over one year at the rate r, $(r \times PV)$, will result in the amount $X at the end of the one-year period. PV is the present value of $X one year in the future, discounted at the rate r.

The superscript notation of 1 in either equation (3.1) or (3.2) refers to the fact that the time horizon is one year in the future.[10] If the time horizon were two years into the future, then the superscript would be 2, and so forth: $(1 + r)^2 = (1 + r) \times (1 + r)$.[11]

If $X is expected to be available in each of the next ten years, for example, then the present value of $X in each of the next ten years, discounted at the rate r, is mathematically equal to:

$$PV = \left[\$X / (1+r)^1 \right] + \left[\$X / (1+r)^2 \right] + \ldots$$
$$+ \left[\$X / (1+r)^9 \right] + \left[\$X / (1+r)^{10} \right] \tag{3.3}$$

To anticipate the application of equation (3.3) for valuation purposes, consider the following very simple illustration. Assume that $X represents the value of a company's expected future net earnings, expected future net income, or whatever financial measure is relevant to determining the value of the company in each of the next ten years. Assume also that this value remains constant in each of the next ten years. Further assume that this company will only be in business for the next ten years and then it will vanish. The valuation question is: what would a willing and fully informed buyer pay today, in the present, to a willing and fully informed seller of a company that is expected to earn $X per year for each of the next ten years? Equation (3.3) provides the answer to this question, assuming that r is the appropriate discount rate (and the economic meaning of r is discussed in more detail below).

To generalize from equation (3.3), the present value of $X in each of the next n years (and in equation (3.3), $n = 10$), discounted at the rate r, is mathematically equal to:

$$PV = \left[\$X/(1+r)^1\right] + \ldots + \left[\$X/(1+r)^n\right] \tag{3.4}$$

A useful mathematical shortcut (presented here without derivation) for calculations like that in equation (3.4), where the time horizon is a finite period of n years, is:

$$PV = \$X\left\{\left[(1+r)^n - 1\right] / \left[r \times (1+r)^n\right]\right\} \tag{3.5}$$

From equation (3.4), if $n = \infty$ (meaning that if $X is assumed to exist each and every year into the infinite future), or more generally if the business being valued is assumed to exist forever and have earnings equal to $X in each and every year, then the present value of this infinite (∞) stream of profits is:

$$PV = \left[\$X / (1+r)^1 \right] + \ldots + \left[\$X / (1+r)^{\infty} \right] \qquad (3.6)$$

Equation (3.6) can be simplified by factoring $X from each term in equation (3.6) to yield:

$$PV = \$X \left\{ \left[1/(1+r)^1 \right] + \ldots + \left[1/(1+r)^{\infty} \right] \right\} \qquad (3.7)$$

The expression in braces in equation (3.7) is mathematically equivalent to $[1/r]$ (presented here without derivation), and the value $[1/r]$ is frequently referred to as the capitalization factor. Given this equivalency, equation (3.7) becomes:[12]

$$PV = \$X \times [1/r], \text{ or } PV = \$X / r \qquad (3.8)$$

The discount rate is r in each of the above present value calculations. When the time horizon is infinite, it is common for the discount rate to be referred to as the capitalization rate or, more simply, using the term *cap rate*. The corresponding capitalization factor is thus the reciprocal of the capitalization rate.

It is important to emphasize that the implicit assumption that underlies capitalization is that $X, or the relevant financial metric of the business being valued, has an infinite life. That is, $X will last forever and always remain at the same value.

Table 3.3 illustrates a present value calculation. It assumes that the future investment, $X, equals $100 in each of the next four years and the discount rate is 5 percent. The calculated present value is $354.60.

Table 3.3 PRESENT VALUE OF $X FOR 4 YEARS BASED ON
EQUATION (3.6) USING A 5% DISCOUNT RATE

Time Period (n=4)	$X	$(1+r)^n$	PV (rounded)
1 (1 year in the future)	$100	$(1+0.05)^1 = 1.05$	$95.24
2 (2 years in the future)	$100	$(1+0.05)^2 = 1.10$	$90.70
3 (3 years in the future)	$100	$(1+0.05)^3 = 1.1576$	$86.38
4 (4 years in the future)	$100	$(1+0.05)^4 = 1.2155$	$82.27
			Sum = $354.60

3.4 RISK ANALYSIS

Determining the discount rate, r, to use in a valuation falls broadly under the heading of risk analysis. Risk is defined as the probability that the actual return on an investment will differ from its expected return. Risk is not good or bad; risk is simply a characterization of the likelihood that future expectations will be realized.[13]

Risk characterizes all business activities, but it is not a characteristic that can easily be quantified. Difficulty aside, risk must be quantified to value any business using a valuation method that is based on a present value calculation, that is, r must be estimated.[14]

Following Link and Boger (1999), the discount rate, r, quantifies the risk of the business. Stated differently, r is the return that could be earned on a comparable alternative investment. This comparable return comprises three parts. The first part is an estimate of the expected future rate of inflation, the second part is what economists call the real rate of interest or the finite return to an investor for sacrificing current purchasing opportunities for future purchasing opportunities, and the third part is a premium for accepting the risk that characterizes the investment. Thus, the comparable return is:

$$r = \text{expected rate of inflation} + \text{real rate of interest}$$
$$+ \text{risk premium} \qquad (3.9)$$

To operationalize equation (3.9), one begins with the risk-free rate of return and the risk-free rate of return combined with the expected rate of inflation and the real rate of interest. Then one increases that percentage to account for the competitive risk, regulatory risk, cost risk, customer risk, marketability risk, and financial risk of the going-concern business being valued.[15]

Volumes have been written about the nuances associated with determining the risk premium to use for the valuation of a specific going-concern business; summarizing all of the arguments, methods, and caveats is beyond the scope of this book. To support the arguments that we present in this book, it is sufficient to simply assume that an appropriate value of r can be calculated and will be used with one of the traditional valuation methods described in the next chapter.

3.5 SUMMARY

We have outlined here four so-called tools of the trade. Forecasting, weighted averages, present value and capitalization, and risk analysis are relevant tools for the valuation of any enterprise, entrepreneurial or not. The following chapters refer explicitly to these tools and to their possible applicability when valuing an entrepreneurial enterprise.

NOTES

1 The valuation tools presented in this chapter are discussed in any valuation book, treatise, or primer. Readily available explanations of each of them are on the Internet. These valuation tools are also fundamental to most college-level text books in accounting, economics, and finance. One source, albeit more technical and prepared for a different audience than this book, is Link and Boger (1999). This chapter draws in large part from that reference.

2 Simple mathematics is involved in our conceptual presentation. We think that foundational concepts should be understood before one uses the tools and valuation methods that the concepts support. For example, to anticipate a discussion in Chapter 5, the use of capitalization to calculate present value is incorrect in the case study presented there, but absent the simple mathematics underlying capitalization that are presented in this chapter, one might not fully understand why.

3 Such an annual time (t) series of data could also be represented as $Y_{t-5}, Y_{t-4}, Y_{t-3}, Y_{t-2}, Y_{t-1},$ and Y_t, where Y_t corresponds to the current year, Y_{t-1} to the previous year, and so forth.

4 Using alternative notation, values of Y for years 7 through 10 could be represented as Y_{t+1} through Y_{t+4}.

5 Most spreadsheet or statistical software packages contain a routine to fit a trend line using a statistical technique known as least squares estimation or least squares regression analysis. The term *least squares* refers to the criterion used in regression analysis to define the best straight line to fit a set of data. Certainly, there are a number of straight lines that can approximate a given set of data. The line for which the sum of squared deviations of actual data from the fitted data (measured vertically and referred to as the error terms) is a minimum defines the least (i.e., minimum) squares regression line, and it is conventionally accepted that the least squares regression line is the best of all possible lines to represent a set of data. Thus, the term *best* refers to a least squares regression line. However, the assumptions that underlie least squares regression analysis, namely that the error terms are randomly distributed around the regression line, might not be valid. When the error terms follow a non-random pattern, autocorrelation is said to exist, and unless this statistical issue is corrected, the resulting estimated intercept and slope coefficients

will be biased. If these estimated coefficients are biased then any forecast that is based on the fitted line will also be biased. For accuracy, a more sophistical regression package might be needed for the correction of autocorrelation.

6   Recall in the example above that all six of the historical data were equally important in the calculation of the trend line.

7   Mathematically, $(5 + 9 + 12 + 10 + 19 + 17)/6 = 12$.

8   Mathematically, a weighted average of a set of data can never be greater than the largest datum.

9   The term *expected* with reference to future values of $\$X$ emphasizes that no forecasting technique will yield values that are accurate *ex post*.

10 If the time horizon were months, for example, then superscript 1 would refer to a one-month period in the future and the discount rate would be equal to a monthly rate of interest that would be approximately equal to one-twelfth of the annual interest rate $(r/12)$.

11 This formula implies that one is also earning interest in year 2 on the interest earned in year 1. The interest is compounding.

12 Equation (3.8) follows logically from equation (3.5). As the time horizon increases, that is, as n increases and approaches ∞, the numerator in the first bracketed expression in equation (3.5) approaches $[(1 + r)^n]$. Thus, the term in braces in equation (3.5) in this limiting situation equals $\{[(1 + r)^n]/(r \times (1 + r)^n)]\}$. After canceling like terms, this expression becomes $[1/r]$.

13 Risk is not the same as uncertainty. Uncertainty characterizes an investment choice for which the investor has no information about the return to be earned on the investment, whereas with risk an estimate can be made about the probabilities associated with the alternative returns.

14 Excellent research, however, has been done by many scholars in an effort to approximate risk, as summarized in Link and Boger (1999).

15 See Table 6.2 in Link and Boger (1999, pp. 65–66) and the related discussion.

4

Traditionally Used
Valuation Methods

This chapter summarizes four traditional valuation methods.[1] Recall that this book is not intended to be a primer on how one conducts a valuation of a closely held business, entrepreneurial or otherwise. Rather, its purpose is to pose, at the conceptual level, how one should think about valuing an entrepreneurial enterprise.

This chapter is divided into four sections. Section 4.1 surveys income-based valuation methods, including the present value of adjusted future net earnings and the price-to-earnings approach. Section 4.2 provides an overview of the asset-based valuation method, followed by a discussion of a hybrid approach in Section 4.3. The chapter concludes with a brief summary statement.

Following the discussion of valuation methods in this chapter, we illustrate how to implement each method in Chapter 5. In Chapters 6, 7, and 8 we critique these traditional valuation methods and thus reject their applicability and relevance for the valuation of an entrepreneurial enterprise.

Most of the valuation methods that are discussed in the academic and professional literatures, and used by practitioners, fall broadly under the heading of an income-based or asset-based approach. There is one exception, and that method is a hybrid of the previous two. Regardless of the valuation method, it is assumed that there is a willing and fully informed seller and a willing and fully informed buyer for the closely held business.

An income-based method relies on the Income Statement of the business or comparable businesses as the starting point for the valuation.[2] Similarly, an asset-based method relies on the Balance Sheet of the business as the starting point.[3] An Income Statement and a Balance Sheet together describe critical dimensions of the financial condition of the company, and thus both are typically examined regardless of the valuation method that is used.

Two fundamental and extremely important assumptions underlie all business valuations. One assumption is that the current financial health of the business is accurately characterized though its financial statements, and the other assumption is that the current financial health of the business is a reasonable starting point for forecasting its future financial health. If the financial statements are incorrectly prepared, or if they overstate or understate the true financial picture of the going concern for some accounting reason(s), it logically follows that the valuation will be inaccurate.[4]

4.1 INCOME-BASED VALUATION METHODS

Two income-based valuation methods are discussed below. The first is the present value of adjusted future net earnings valuation method and the second is the price-to-earnings ratio valuation method.

Present Value of Adjusted Future Net Earnings

Underlying the present value of adjusted future net earnings or adjusted future net income method is the assumption that the to-be-valued aspect of the business being sold is its ability to generate future earnings for the potential buyer. The buyer is thus attempting to value the business in terms of a claim to a future stream of earnings.[5]

A critical factor in this method of analysis is how far into the future a reasonable and fully informed buyer will look when determining the set of relevant information to use to arrive at the present value of the business. That is, would a buyer look to purchasing a five-year, ten-year, or infinite stream of net earnings (to list only a few of the possibilities)? If it is justifiable to impose a specific rather than indefinite time period, then the valuation method is centered around taking the present value of adjusted future net earnings (AFE) based on the Income Statement and other information, and using a formula analogous to that developed in equations (3.4) and (3.5):

$$PV = \left[\$AFE / (1+r)^1 \right] + \ldots + \left[\$AFE / (1+r)^n \right] or$$
$$PV = \$AFE \left\{ \left[(1+r)^n - 1 \right] / \left[r \times (1+r)^n \right] \right\} \tag{4.1}$$

Or, if the valuator believes that the buyer is purchasing an infinite stream of adjusted future earnings, the relevant formula is analogous to the capitalization formula developed in equation (3.8):

$$PV = \$AFE / r \tag{4.2}$$

The term *adjusted future net earnings* requires an explanation. Specifically, the adjectives *adjusted* and *future* need to be elaborated on because unadjusted and current net earnings, or net income, are reported on the Income Statement. Adjustments to net earnings on the Income Statement are intended to approximate what the Income Statement would look like if the business were owned and operated by an average potential buyer. That is, the adjustments to the Income Statement are intended to remove any unique revenue-generating abilities, costs (e.g., charitable donations), or accounting procedures that are specific to the seller's management style. After such adjustments are made—that is, after the Income Statement has been normalized—current net earnings reported on it will be used to approximate all future net earnings. In other words, current adjusted net earnings, or a weighted average of current and past adjusted net earnings, will be used to estimate—generally without a premium factor for future growth—the net earnings a buyer can expect to earn under new ownership and management.[6]

If equation (4.1) is used for the present value calculation, it is explicitly assumed that the business's earnings life will be n years. If equation (4.2) is used for the capitalization calculation, it is explicitly assumed that the business's net earnings life will be infinite.

If a limited earnings life is a reasonable assumption for the to-be-valued business, then it is also reasonable to assume that after n years the business will have some residual value. In other words, after n years there will be a value to the remaining assets of the business. Estimating the residual value of a business is subjective and thus a subject of debate when a buy/sell agreement is being negotiated. To avoid this element of debate, adjusted future earnings are often capitalized. This approach assumes that the life of the business is infinite regardless of who the future owner might be.

Regarding the specific adjustments to the Income Statement, a potential buyer could view net earnings or net income as an over- or understatement of the net earnings or net income that might exist in the future during his or her ownership and management. One adjustment that is frequently considered relates to the seller's or current owner's compensation. Is the current owner paid more or less than the buyer would be paid or than would be needed to hire a manager to assume all of the responsibilities of the current owner? Adjusting the Income Statement for owner's compensation,[7] or for any other appropriate circumstances, is done to reflect the buyer's perceived ability to operate the company.

Once the Income Statement has been normalized, another adjustment is often needed to complete the calculation of the fair market value of the company. This adjustment is referred to as a marketability adjustment. Whereas the discount rate or capitalization rate used in a fairmarket valuation reflects the risk of operating the business, a transfer adjustment rate reflects the risk and uncertainty of being able to actually sell the business in a real world arm's-length transaction in a timely manner, rather than under a hypothetical scenario.[8] This marketability adjustment— more precisely, an adjustment for *lack* of marketability—applies to all valuations of closely held businesses regardless of the valuation method used; no business is likely to sell immediately.[9]

Thus, the steps to follow when using a present value of adjusted future net earnings method are the following: determine the expected life of the business—a limited life of *n* years or an indefinite life; estimate an appropriate discount rate, *r*; normalize the Income Statement; calculate a weighted average of adjusted future net earnings, assuming that it is appropriate; calculate the present value of the weighted average of adjusted future earnings using either the limited life present value equation (4.1), to which a residual value for the business must then be added, or the capitalization equation (4.2); and finally adjust for marketability as appropriate (see Table 4.1).

Table 4.1 PRESENT VALUE OF ADJUSTED FUTURE NET
EARNINGS VALUATION METHOD

Steps	Procedure
1	Determine the expected life of the business—a limited life of n years or an indefinite life.
2	Estimate an appropriate discount rate, r.
3	Normalize the Income Statement.
4	Calculate a weighted average of adjusted future net earnings, assuming that a weighted average of adjusted future net earnings is appropriate.
5	Calculate the present value of the weighted average of adjusted future net earnings using either the limited life present value equation (4.1), to which a residual value for the business must then be added, or the capitalization equation (4.2).
6	Adjust for marketability as appropriate.

Price-to-Earnings Ratio

The present value of adjusted future net earnings method described above relies on information reported on the business's Income Statement as well as on comparable industry information for adjustments. The price-to-earnings ratio valuation method relies on the same two sources of information.[10]

The assumption underlying the price-to-earnings method is that the fair market value of the closely held business can be approximated from the market value of comparable publicly traded companies. To implement this method, the valuator must be able to identify a set of presumed-to-be-comparable publicly traded companies and obtain sufficient information on each to verify the extent of comparability from an economic, management, and financial perspective. No publicly traded company will be precisely comparable to the closely held business being valued, so informed judgment must be exercised.[11]

Publicly traded companies are relatively large in terms of sales, revenues or assets when compared to a small closely held company. Moreover, publicly traded companies are diversified across product lines. This diversification implies that reported revenues are from various lines of business, not all of which are relevant for comparative purposes. Also, diversification reduces the operating risk of the company, and to the extent that this reduced risk is reflected in the company's realized net earnings and in the publicly reported price, the comparison is likely less than accurate. Most small closely held companies are not diversified, and this characteristic alone makes financial comparisons difficult.[12]

Comparability is a difficult concept to define, much less to quantify accurately. Certainly, informed individuals—including buyers and sellers—will have differing opinions about what is and is not comparable. One reason for these differences is asymmetry of information. The valuation is conducted under the assumption that both the buyer and seller are fully informed individuals. This fair market value assumption is a construct; in reality, such is rarely the case. The seller will know the nuances of the business, such as the personalities of its customers or its suppliers, and the buyer will have preconceived ideas about the business's future capabilities. Still, there are systematic methods of comparing dimensions of the to-be-valued business with other businesses. The methods fall under the rubric of a ratio analysis. The more frequently used financial ratios that are available from public and private sources and that can be compared to calculable ratios for the to-be-valued company are liquidity ratios, capital structure ratios, and profitability ratios.[13]

Regarding the mechanics of the price-to-earnings ratio valuation method, the ratio of the to-be-valued business's adjusted future net earnings (AFE), or adjusted net income, to its number of shares of stock outstanding (S) is first calculated. The number of shares outstanding is reported in the company's financial statements. This ratio for the business being valued is $(AFE/S)_{business}$. Having identified a comparable company or set of comparable companies,[14] the average price-to-earnings ratio for one share of the comparable company's stock is $(P/E)_{comparable}$.

It follows that the market-based price per share of the business being valued, $(P/S)_{market,}$ equals the product of the business's adjusted future earnings-to-shares ratio, $(AFE/S)_{business,}$ and the comparable price-to-earnings ratio, $(P/E)_{comparable,}$ as:

$$(P/S)_{market} = (E/S)_{business} \times (P/E)_{comparable} \qquad (4.3)$$

It also follows that the market-based price or value of the business being considered is the product of the business's adjusted future earnings and the price-to-earnings ratio of comparable companies, as:[15]

$$P_{market} = AFE_{business} \times (P/E)_{comparable} \qquad (4.4)$$

In equation (4.4), P_{market} represents the market-based price or value of the closely held company being valued. Stated differently, P_{market} is determined on the basis of the ratio of market prices to earnings from a comparable company or set of comparable companies. Market prices from publicly held companies may be a reasonable proxy for the value of a closely held company if the companies are comparable and if the market-based price is adjusted for the fact that publicly held companies are readily marketable and closely held companies are not. Thus, the price determined from equation (4.4) must be adjusted to account for the fact that the closely held company is less marketable than the publicly held companies from which P_{market} was derived.[16]

Assume there is only one comparable publicly traded company. When the publicly traded company's information is used for comparative purposes, the price, P, in the price-to-earnings ratio, $(P/E)_{comparable}$, is the price of one share of traded stock. Hence, it represents the price of a minority ownership share. To value a majority position in a closely held company based on a minority ownership share from a publicly traded company requires that a premium be added to the final valuation estimate.[17] To the best of our knowledge there is no theoretical basis or related academic or practitioner literature on the precise size of this ownership adjustment or on its variability by type of business (e.g., by industry or sector) being valued. The magnitude of this adjustment is, in practice, simply a matter of the valuator's expert opinion.

Thus, the steps to follow when using a price-to-earnings ratio valuation method are to identify a publicly traded company or set of publicly traded companies and calculate a price-to-earnings ratio, $(P/E)_{comparable}$; normalize the Income Statement to determine $AFE_{business}$; multiply the above two values and then adjust the product by a publicly traded marketability discount; and finally adjust by an ownership premium (see Table 4.2).

Table 4.2 PRICE-TO-EARNINGS RATIO VALUATION METHOD

Steps	Procedure
1	Identify a publicly traded company or set of publicly traded companies and calculate a price-to-earnings ratio, $(P/E)_{comparable}$.
2	Normalize the Income Statement to determine $AFE_{business}$.
3	Multiply the above two values, and then adjust the product by a publicly traded marketability discount.
4	Adjust by an ownership premium.

4.2 ASSET-BASED VALUATION METHOD

The value of the business's net assets is a lower bound on the going-concern fair market value of the business. It is our opinion that an asset-based valuation method is most appropriate if the business is being liquidated. This method yields a lower bound on the fair market value of the company because it assumes that all assets are being sold rather than being used to generate any future value for the company.

Implementing an asset-based valuation method is relatively straightforward. The valuator adjusts the assets on the Balance Sheet to their economic or market values, often with the assistance of an outside and presumably unbiased appraiser, and then the valuator subtracts total liabilities from these adjusted total assets to arrive at adjusted net assets.

It should be emphasized that assets as reflected on the Balance Sheet are not intended to be representative of the current (at the time of the valuation) economic value of assets. Balance Sheets

Table 4.3 ADJUSTED NET ASSET VALUATION METHOD

Steps	Procedure
1	Adjust the Balance Sheet to reflect the fair market value of assets.
2	Determine the value of goodwill, if any.
3	Subtract total liabilities from adjusted total assets to arrive at adjusted net assets.
4	Adjust for marketability as appropriate.

prepared in accordance with GAAP reflect the cost of assets at the time of acquisition, not at their economic or current fair market value. While circumstances will dictate what adjustments to the value of assets are needed, the more common adjustments account for a percentage of accounts receivable not being collectable, fair market value of real property, and the market value of goodwill.[18]

Thus, the steps to follow when using the adjusted net asset valuation method are to adjust the Balance Sheet to reflect the fair market value of assets; determine the value of goodwill, if any; subtract total liabilities from adjusted total assets to arrive at adjusted net assets; and adjust for transfer marketability as appropriate (see Table 4.3).

4.3 INCOME-BASED AND ASSET-BASED VALUATION METHOD

The capitalization of excess earnings approach is a widely practiced method for valuing a going concern, although its historical origins clearly show that it was not intended for that use. This method was designed only for the valuation of the intangible assets of a going concern.[19]

The steps to follow when using the capitalization of excess earnings method are to calculate a weighted average of adjusted future net earnings, or adjusted future net income, from the Income Statement; calculate a weighted average of the market value of tangible assets from the Balance Sheet; determine an expected return on the weighted average of the market value of tangible assets; subtract the return expected on these tangible assets from the weighted average of adjusted future net earnings to determine excess earnings; capitalize excess earnings; and add to the capitalized value of excess earnings the fair market value of current tangible assets and adjust the sum for ownership control and marketability (see Table 4.4).

All of the values that are needed to implement the capitalization of excess earnings valuation method are available from the company's financial statements or from informed opinions. In practice, regarding step 3 in Table 4.4, it is common for a valuator to impute a risk-free rate of interest to determine the expected return on the weighted average of the market value of tangible assets. The specific risk-free rate of interest to use for this calculation is generally determined on the basis of the valuator's expert opinion, but the choice should be consistent with the other implicit assumptions of this valuation method. Specifically, when excess earnings are being capitalized in step 5, the valuator is assuming that the business has an infinite life. Recall that this assumption follows directly from equations (3.8) and (4.2). Thus, a long-term risk free rate of interest (e.g., the rate of interest on a long-term Treasury bond as of the date of the valuation) might be the most appropriate rate to use.

Table 4.4 CAPITALIZATION OF EXCESS EARNINGS
VALUATION METHOD

Steps	Procedure
1	Calculate a weighted average of adjusted future net earnings from the Income Statement.
2	Calculate a weighted average of the market value of tangible assets from the Balance Sheet.
3	Determine an expected return on the weighted average of the market value of tangible assets.
4	Subtract the return expected on these tangible assets from the weighted average of adjusted future earnings to determine excess earnings.
5	Capitalize excess earnings.
6	Add to the capitalized value of excess earnings the fair market value of current tangible assets and adjust the sum for marketability as appropriate.

4.4. SUMMARY

This chapter summarized several traditional valuation methods. While our descriptions of how to implement each were simplistic, our intent was only to set the stage for later chapters. For completeness, we illustrate how to estimate fair market value using each method in the following chapter. Chapter 5 thus becomes the straw man for the chapters that follow. In those following chapters we argue that traditional valuation methods are not applicable when valuing an entrepreneurial enterprise.

NOTES

1   The valuation methods presented and discussed in this chapter can be found in any valuation book, treatise, or primer. A readily available explanation and illustration of each is likely on the Internet. These valuation methods are also fundamental to most college-level text books in accounting and finance. One source, albeit more technical and prepared for a different audience than this book, is Link and Boger (1999). This chapter draws in large part from that reference.

2   An Income Statement is part of a business's overall financial statements. It presents the results of operations for an accounting period or fiscal year.

3   A Balance Sheet is a report that shows the financial position of a business at a particular point in time. Assets are shown in the order of their liquidity, and liabilities are shown in the order of their maturity date.

4   It is generally the case that individuals trained in Generally Accepted Accounting Principles (GAAP) are involved in some way in the preparation of a business's financial statements. A Certified Public Accountant's (CPA) involvement with the business's financial statements can be detailed or minimal. Financial statements are accordingly characterized in terms of the level of such involvement: audited, reviewed, or compiled. An audited financial statement reflects the highest level of involvement by an independent CPA. If a statement is audited, the auditor has stated an opinion that the financial statements are presented in conformity with GAAP. The second level of involvement is called a review engagement. A reviewed financial statement is one for which the CPA has a reasonable basis for expressing limited assurance that there are no material modifications needed to make the financial statement conform to GAAP. Finally, a compiled financial statement is one for which the CPA has taken the information provided by the owner or management of the business and simply presented it in a generally accepted format without any representation as to its accuracy.

5   A relevant issue is whether the valuation should be conducted on a pre-tax or an after-tax basis. The valuation profession differs with regard to this issue, and there is no definitive right or wrong answer. What is important is for all parties to understand the underlying assumptions being brought to the valuation and for all parties to verify that the data used in the valuation process are consistent. For simplicity, we are proceeding in this chapter on a pre-tax basis.

6   Because a weighted average of past adjusted net earnings is generally used in the present value calculation within the adjusted future net earnings valuation method, one should not infer that a weighted average is appropriate in all situations. For example, if there is a reason to believe that net earnings are expected to increase in the future, then a weighted average of past values of net earnings may not be the most appropriate base to use to approximate future net earnings.

7   Frequently, published information on comparable compensations is used for this adjustment.

8   The term *arm's-length transaction* refers to neither the buyer nor the seller being under any compulsion to buy or sell the business.

9   Another adjustment to the calculated value of the business is relevant if there are several owners of the business and one owner wants to sell his or her shares to one of the other owners or to an outside party. The logic of this ownership adjustment or ownership premium adjustment is as follows. If there are, say, three equal owners, one owner's share is 33.33% of the calculated fair market value of the business. An ownership control premium should be added to this 33.33% amount to account for the fact that the prospective equal ownership share buyer is not only purchasing the future earnings capabilities of the business but also the ability to influence the future direction of the business and thus possibly its future earnings. If the 33.33% ownership is not being sold to an outside party but rather to one of the other owners, that owner will then gain a controlling interest in the company, having a 66.66% ownership share after the sale. This too will increase the worth of the share of the company being valued because the new owner will have majority ownership control over the direction of the business.

10 Some may not view the price-to-earnings method as falling under the category of an income-based valuation method. An alternative would be to classify it under a third heading called, say, the comparable method. We do not have trouble with the latter type of classification, but we prefer to discuss the price-to-earnings ratio method as an income-based method because it is the net earnings or net income of publicly traded companies that are relevant for this valuation analysis.

11 There are many sources for information on publicly traded companies including information provided by, for example, Value Line and Standard and Poor's.

12 As a general rule, the smaller the size and the more limited the scope of activities of the business being valued, the less likely there will be a set of publicly traded companies that are comparable, or even a single publicly traded company that is comparable.

13 Definitions of these widely known and widely used comparability ratios are available from many places, including college-level text books in accounting

and finance. These ratios are also discussed on many Internet sites. One useful source is the *Annual Statement Studies* prepared by Robert Morris Associates (RMA). An abbreviated explanation of these ratios is also in Link and Boger (1999). Many of the ratios below approximate similar characteristics of the financial nature of the company.

Under the heading of Liquidity Ratios:

- Current Ratio = (Current Assets/Current Liabilities). This ratio measures the company's ability to pay its debts in the short term.
- Acid-Test Ratio = (Securities + Receivables/Current Liabilities). This ratio also measures the company's ability to pay its debts in the short term.
- Cash Ratio = (Cash/Current Liabilities). This ratio measures the company's ability to pay its debts in the very short term.
- Receivables Turnover Ratio = (Net Sales/Average Net Receivables). This ratio is a measure of how efficient the company is in collecting its receivables, thus it measures how efficient the company is in managing its credit.
- Age of Receivables Ratio = (365/Receivables Turnover Ratio). This ratio is a measure of how efficient the company is in controlling credit and collections.
- Inventory Turnover Ratio = (Cost of Goods Sold/Average Inventory). This ratio is a measure of the marketability of the company's ability to manage its inventory.
- Days in Inventory Ratio = (365/Inventory Ratio). This ratio is a measure that approximates the average length of time needed to sell inventory.
- Working Capital Turnover Ratio = (Net Sales/Average Working Capital). This ratio is a measure of how effectively the company uses its working capital to generate sales.
- Number of Days' Purchases in Ending Accounts Payable = (Accounts Payable/Average Daily Purchases). This ratio is a measure of how promptly the company pays its bills.

Under the heading of Capital Structure Ratios:

- Owner's Equity to Total Assets Ratio = (Total Owners' Equity/Total Net Assets). This ratio is a measure of the owner's asset contribution to the company.
- Owner's Equity to Total Liabilities Ratio = (Total Owner's Equity/Total Liabilities). This ratio is a measure of the claims that both owners and creditors have on the company.
- Fixed Assets to Total Equity Ratio = (Total Owner's Equity/Fixed Net Assets). This ratio is a measure of the extent to which the owner's capital is available as working capital for the company.

- Book Value per Share of Common Stock Ratio = (Common Equity Stock/ Number of Shares of Common Stock). This ratio is a measure of net assets as reported on the financial statement per share of common stock.
- Total Liabilities to Total Assets Ratio = (Total Liabilities/Total Net Assets). This ratio is a measure of the extent of protection the company has against creditors; it also is a measure of the extent to which the company is operating on equity.
- Total Liabilities to Owners' Equity Ratio = (Total Liabilities/Owners' Equity). This ratio is a measure of the relationship between what the company owes and what the company owns.

Under the heading of Profitability Ratios:

- Net Income to Sales Ratio = (Net Income/Net Sales). This ratio is a measure of the company's profit margin per dollar of sales.
- Operation Ratio = (Cost of Goods Sold + Operating Expenses/Net Sales). This ratio is a measure of the company's profit margin per dollar of sales.
- Asset Turnover Ratio = (Net Sales/Average Total Assets). This ratio is a measure of how productive the company's assets are in generating sales.
- Earnings per Share of Common Stock Ratio = ((Net Income - Preferred Dividend Requirements)/Number of Share of Common Stock). This ratio is a measure of the return on common stockholder's investments per share of common stock.
- Price-to-Earnings Ratio = (Market Price per Share of Common Stock/ Net Earnings or Net Income per Share of Common Stock). This ratio is a measure of the market price of a share of common stock.
- Dividend Yield Ratio = (Cash Dividends per Share of Common Stock/ Market Price per Share of Common Stock). This ratio is a measure of the return or cash yield on a share of common stock.
- Return on Assets Ratio = (Net Earnings or Net Income/Total Assets). This ratio is a measure of the return or yield on total assets.
- Return on Stockholder's Common Equity Ratio = (Net Earnings or Net Income/Stockholder's Common Equity). This ratio is a measure of the return or yield on stockholder's common stock investments.
- Payout Ratio = (Cash Dividends/Net Earnings or Net Income). This ratio is a measure of the distribution of current earning to stockholders.
- Cash Flow from Operations per Share of Common Stock Ratio = (Net Earnings or Net Income Adjusted for Non-Cash Items/Number of Shares of Common Stock). This ratio is a measure of the cash generated by the company per share of common stock.

14 In practice, one would typically identify several comparable public companies and then average their price-to-earnings-ratios.

15 Equation (4.4) follows from equation (4.3) by multiplying both sides of equation (4.3) by S.

16 There are sources of information that a valuator can refer to for guidance on the appropriate publicly traded marketability discount—discount for lack of marketability would be a more accurate phrase, although not the one that the profession uses—but the relevance of these sources for a particular valuation is questionable.

17 The purpose of an ownership control adjustment is to account for the fact that a buyer is purchasing not only the current earning capabilities of the closely held business but also the ability to influence its future direction. This is not the case when shares of a publicly traded company are purchased.

18 Goodwill is a non-operating intangible asset of some businesses. Conceptually, it represents the earning power of a business above the normal rate of return on net assets for the industry in which the business operates.

19 The origin of the concept of capitalizing excess earnings traces to the U.S. Treasury Department's "Appeals and Revenue Memorandum Number 34" (A.R.M. 34). A.R.M. 34 was issued in 1920 for the purpose of determining the amount of March 1, 1913 intangible asset value lost by breweries and other businesses connected with the distilling industry as a result of the passage of the Eighteenth Amendment to the Constitution of the United States. Aspects of A.R.M. 34 were clarified that same year by A.R.M. 68, but more importantly this "formula" approach to the fair market value of intangible assets was qualified in Revenue Ruling 68–908, and the debate continues today as to the relevance of the capitalization of excess earnings approach to valuation.

5

Applications of Traditional
Valuation Methods

This chapter illustrates the calculation of the fair market value of a hypothetical business called Business, Inc. The Income Statement and the Balance Sheet of this company are used to illustrate the application of each of the four traditional valuation methods presented in Chapter 4. The dollar values within these two financial statements are, of course, constructed, as are the other numerical values used in this chapter. Our purpose in demonstrating the application of these methods is to emphasize their assumptions and therefore their inherent limitations for use when valuing an entrepreneurial enterprise.

As discussed in previous chapters, information beyond what is reported on the Income Statement and Balance Sheet is needed in the calculations of value through each method. This information is related to, among other things, an adjustment of owner's compensation to normalize the Income Statement, a discount or capitalization rate, a marketability discount factor, and an ownership control premium if appropriate. We simply assume values for these variables and offer no derivation or explanation because each is tangential to the purpose at hand.

The Income Statement and the Balance Sheet for Business, Inc. are in Tables 5.1 and 5.2.

Table 5.1 BUSINESS, INC. INCOME STATEMENT

	2005	2006	2007	2008	2009
Revenues:					
Sales	$1,000,000	$1,265,000	$1,572,000	$1,803,000	$1,992,000
Operating Expenses:					
Cost of Goods	358,000	419,000	499,000	578,000	623,000
Owner's Compensation	150,000	175,000	209,000	299,000	355,000
Other Salaries	225,000	368,000	407,000	509,000	621,000
Payroll Taxes	40,000	46,000	52,000	69,000	83,000

Profit Sharing Plan	20,000	23,000	26,000	34,500	41,500
Misc. Supplies	10,000	12,000	15,000	18,000	21,000
Depreciation	20,000	25,000	30,000	35,000	40,000
Rent	75,000	85,000	95,000	105,000	115,000
Insurance	22,000	28,000	32,000	38,000	42,000
Other Expenses	42,000	38,000	149,000	131,500	49,460
Total Operating Expenses	$962,000	$1,219,000	$1,514,000	$1,817,000	$1,990,960
Net Earnings (Net Income)	$38,000	$46,000	$58,000	($14,000)	$1,040

Table 5.2 BUSINESS, INC. BALANCE SHEET

	2005	2006	2007	2008	2009
Current Assets:					
Cash	$ 25,000	$ 65,000	$105,000	$115,000	$ 75,000
Inventory	250,000	300,000	336,000	349,000	314,000
Prepaid Expenses	2,500	2,500	2,500	2,500	2,500
Total Current Assets	277,500	367,500	443,500	466,500	391,500
Property and Equipment:					
Leasehold Improvements	250,000	300,000	340,000	370,000	390,000
Office Furniture and Equipment	95,000	140,000	155,000	170,000	185,000
Accumulated Depreciation	(75,000)	(105,000)	(140,000)	(180,000)	(225,000)

Total Property and Equipment	270,000	335,000	355,000	360,000	350,000
Total Assets	$547,500	$702,500	$798,500	$826,500	$741,500
Current Liabilities:					
Accounts Payable	$200,000	$220,000	$242,000	$266,000	$293,000
Bank Loan	175,000	190,000	205,000	220,000	235,000
Accrued Salaries	15,000	16,000	17,000	18,000	19,000
Accrued Profit Sharing Contribution	30,000	32,000	34,000	36,000	38,000
Other Accrued Liabilities	15,000	15,000	15,000	15,000	15,000
Total Current Liabilities	435,000	473,000	513,000	555,000	600,000

(Continued)

Table 5.2 CONTINUED

	2005	2006	2007	2008	2009
Stockholders' Equity:					
Common Stock	10,000	10,000	10,000	10,000	10,000
Retained Earnings	102,500	219,500	275,500	261,500	131,500
Total Stockholders' Equity	112,500	229,500	285,500	271,500	141,500
Total Liabilities and Equity	$547,500	$702,500	$798,500	$826,500	$741,500

The remainder of this chapter is divided into five sections. Sections 5.1 and 5.2 illustrate two income-based valuation methods: the present value of adjusted future net earnings and the price-to-earnings ratio. The asset-based method is presented in Section 5.3, and the hybrid capitalization of excess earnings method is in Section 5.4. Section 5.5 concludes the chapter with a brief summary statement.

5.1 PRESENT VALUE OF ADJUSTED FUTURE NET EARNINGS

In this example, an infinite life is assumed for the business. Thus, the present value of adjusted future net earnings, or the present value of adjusted future net income, will be capitalized to determine the fair market value of Business, Inc.

Regarding adjustments to the Income Statement in Table 5.1, assume the buyer is of the opinion that the current owner's compensation is $50,000 above market value in each of the five years shown. Adjusting the values for owner's compensation in the Income Statement down in each year by $50,000 will decrease total operating expenses in each year by that same amount. And thus net earnings will increase in each year by $50,000. No other adjustments are made to the Income Statement. The normalized Income Statement is in Table 5.3, with adjustments shown in italics.

A discount rate is needed to capitalize any numerical variable—in this case, adjusted future net earnings. The discount rate selected should approximate the future risk of the business, taking into account competitive risk, regulatory risk, cost risk, marketability risk, and financial risk. In other words, the discount rate the valuator chooses should approximate the return that a buyer could earn in an alternative investment of equal risk as Business, Inc.

Table 5.3 BUSINESS, INC. ADJUSTED INCOME STATEMENT

	2005	2006	2007	2008	2009
Revenues:					
Sales	$1,000,000	$1,265,000	$1,572,000	$1,803,000	$1,992,000
Operating Expenses:					
Cost of Goods	358,000	419,000	499,000	578,000	623,000
Owner's Compensation	100,000	125,000	159,000	249,000	305,000
Other Salaries	225,000	368,000	407,000	509,000	621,000
Payroll Taxes	40,000	46,000	52,000	69,000	83,000
Profit Sharing Plan	20,000	23,000	26,000	34,500	41,500

Misc. Supplies	10,000	12,000	15,000	18,000	21,000
Depreciation	20,000	25,000	30,000	35,000	40,000
Rent	75,000	85,000	95,000	105,000	115,000
Insurance	22,000	28,000	32,000	38,000	42,000
Other Expenses	42,000	38,000	149,000	131,500	49,460
Total Operating Expenses	*$912,000*	*$1,169,000*	*$1,464,000*	*$1,767,000*	*$1,940,960*
Adjusted Net Earnings (Adjusted Net Income)	*$88,000*	*$96,000*	*$108,000*	*$36,000*	*$51,040*

Note: The entries in the Income Statement that have changed, compared to the Income Statement in Table 5.1, due to the reduction in owner's compensation by $50,000 per year, are shown by italics.

For Business, Inc., a 25 percent discount rate is assumed to be appropriate. Using a 5–4–3–2–1 weighting scheme for adjusted future net earnings, which is conventional when five years of data are available and is also assumed to be appropriate for this illustration, the weighted average of adjusted future net earnings is $66,880.[1] Based on a discount rate of 25 percent, the present value of the weighted average of adjusted net earnings is $267,520.[2]

No ownership control adjustment is needed because the entire business is being valued for sale, but a 10 percent marketability discount is assumed to be appropriate. After adjusting by the 10 percent marketability discount, the estimated fair market value of Business, Inc. as of the end of 2009 is $240,768.[3]

Table 5.4, which is based on Table 4.1, summarizes the above calculations.

5.2 PRICE-TO-EARNINGS RATIO

The price-to-earnings ratio valuation method is based on the ability of the buyer or seller to identify a comparable set of publicly traded companies.[4] For Business, Inc., assume that a sample of publicly traded companies was identified in 2009 and assume the average (P/E) calculated from the identified sample is 3.2.

This ratio is imputed to the normalized net earnings of the company for 2009. Thus, the value for adjusted net earnings on the Adjusted Income Statement in Table 5.3 for 2009 is relevant for this illustration. In other words, the price-to-earnings valuation method implicitly assumes that only current adjusted net earnings are relevant in the determination of fair market value. Following from the present value of adjusted future net earnings valuation example above, the only adjustment to the company's

Table 5.4 PRESENT VALUE OF ADJUSTED FUTURE NET EARNINGS
VALUATION METHOD

Steps	Procedure	Comments
1	Determine the expected life of the business—a limited life of n years or an indefinite life.	In this example an infinite life of the business is assumed.
2	Estimate an appropriate discount rate, r.	Building on a risk-free rate of 6% and taking into account competitive risk, regulatory risk, cost risk, marketability risk, and financial risk, the appropriate discount rate is assumed to be 25%.
3	Normalize the Income Statement.	The buyer is assumed to adjust the Income Statement for excess owner's or officer's compensation by $50,000 per year. This adjustment is tantamount to increasing net earnings on the Income Statement by $50,000 per year. No other adjustments are made to the Income Statement.

(*Continued*)

Table 5.4 CONTINUED

Steps	Procedure	Comments
4	Calculate a weighted average of adjusted net earnings assuming that a weighted average of adjusted net earnings is appropriate.	Using a 5–4–3–2–1 weighting scheme, the weighted average of adjusted net earnings is $66,880.
5	Calculate the present value of the weighted average of adjusted net earnings using either the limited life present value equation (4.1), to which a residual value for the business must then be added, or the capitalization equation (4.2).	Based on a discount rate of 25%, the present value of the weighted average of adjusted net earnings is $267,520.
6	Adjust for marketability as appropriate.	No ownership control adjustment is needed because the entire business is being valued for sale, but a 10% marketability discount is appropriate. Thus, the fair market value of Business, Inc. as of the end of 2009 is $240,768.

Income Statement for 2009 is to reduce owner's compensation by $50,000; adjusted net earnings for that year are thus $51,040, as shown in Table 5.3.

Imputing a 3.2 price-to-earnings ratio to adjusted net earning yields a gross fair market value of $163,328 to Business, Inc.[5] Adjusting downward by a 10 percent marketability discount yields an adjusted fair market value of $146,995.[6] Adjusting this latter value upward by an assumed 15 percent ownership premium to take into account that the price-to-earnings ratio valuation method is based on a single minority share of stock in a publicly traded company yields a final, fully adjusted fair market value of $169,044 for Business, Inc. as of the end of 2009.[7]

Table 5.5 summarizes the above calculations.

The price-to-earnings ratio valuation method produced a fair market value of Business Inc. $71,724, or nearly 30 percent, lower than the present value of future net earnings valuation method.[8] This conclusion is not unique to the specific Income Statement examples in Tables 5.1 or 5.3. Rather, this result will occur whenever there is a decreasing trend in actual or adjusted net earnings. Note that in Table 5.1, net earnings peaked in 2007, they were negative in 2008, and they were barely positive in 2009. A similar trend can be seen with adjusted net earnings in Table 5.3. Even with the adjustment for owner's compensation, adjusted net earnings in 2009 were lower than the weighted average of adjusted net earnings for the five-year period.

5.3 ADJUSTED NET ASSET VALUATION METHOD

Recall that the adjusted net asset valuation method is most applicable when the business is being valued for the purpose of liquidation

Table 5.5 PRICE-TO-EARNINGS RATIO VALUATION METHOD

Steps	Procedure	Comments
1	Identify a publicly traded company or set of publicly traded companies and calculate a price-to-earnings ratio, $(P/E)_{comparable}$.	In this example, assume that a sample of publicly traded companies was identified in 2009 and the average (P/E) from the sample is 3.2.
2	Normalize the Income Statement to determine $AFE_{business}$.	From the Income Statement, the financial data for 2009 are normalized by reducing owner's compensation by $50,000; thus, adjusted net earnings are $51,040.
3	Multiply the above two values and then adjust the product by a publicly traded marketability discount.	3.2 × $51,040 = $163,328, and adjusting downward by a 10% marketability discount yields $146,995.
4	Adjust by an ownership premium.	A 15% ownership premium is added the value above to arrive at a fair market value of Business, Inc. of $169,044 as of the end of 2009.

or when the business is being sold for the fair market value of its net assets. For this illustration, one adjustment is made to the Balance Sheet in Table 5.2 with respect to inventories. The economics of this assumption is that the value of the company's inventory on its Balance Sheet in Table 5.2 represents worth at the time of acquisition, not at a current fair market value. In reality, most company's inventories will be adjusted downward; for Business, Inc., inventories are adjusted downward by $20,000 in each year (see Table 5.6 and the italicized adjustments therein). Also, assume that Business, Inc. has no goodwill.

The adjusted net asset valuation method relies only on the 2009 total stockholders' equity, which is the difference between total assets and total current liabilities. For 2009, stockholders' equity as reported on the Adjusted Balance Sheet is $121,500.

Adjusting stockholders' equity down by a 10 percent marketability discount yields a fair market value of Business, Inc. of $109,350.[9] This liquidation value of Business, Inc. is, as expected, lower than the price-to-earnings ratio valuation of $169,044.

Table 5.7, which is based on Table 4.3, summarizes the above calculations.

5.4 CAPITALIZATION OF EXCESS EARNINGS VALUATION METHOD

The capitalization of excess earnings valuation method incorporates information from both the Adjusted Income Statement and the Adjusted Balance Sheet. It begins with a calculated weighted average of adjusted future net earnings from the Adjusted Income Statement in Table 5.3. This value is $66,880, as previously calculated and shown in Table 5.4.

Table 5.6 BUSINESS, INC. ADJUSTED BALANCE SHEET

	2005	2006	2007	2008	2009
Current Assets:					
Cash	$ 25,000	$ 65,000	$105,000	$115,000	$ 75,000
Inventory	230,000	280,000	316,000	329,000	294,000
Prepaid Expenses	2,500	2,500	2,500	2,500	2,500
Total Current Assets	257,500	347,500	423,500	446,500	371,500
Property and Equipment:					
Leasehold Improvements	250,000	300,000	340,000	370,000	390,000
Office Furniture and Equipment	95,000	140,000	155,000	170,000	185,000
Accumulated Depreciation	(75,000)	(105,000)	(140,000)	(180,000)	(225,000)
Total Property and Equipment	270,000	335,000	355,000	360,000	350,000
Total Assets	$527,500	$682,500	$778,500	$806,500	$721,500

Current Liabilities:

Accounts Payable	$200,000	$220,000	$242,000	$266,000	$293,000
Bank Loan	175,000	190,000	205,000	220,000	235,000
Accrued Salaries	15,000	16,000	17,000	18,000	19,000
Accrued Profit Sharing Contribution	30,000	32,000	34,000	36,000	38,000
Other Accrued Liabilities	15,000	15,000	15,000	15,000	15,000
Total Current Liabilities	435,000	473,000	513,000	555,000	600,000
Stockholders' Equity:					
Common Stock	10,000	10,000	10,000	10,000	10,000
Retained Earnings	*82,500*	*199,500*	*255,500*	*241,500*	*111,500*
Total Stockholders' Equity	*92,500*	*209,500*	*265,500*	*251,500*	*121,500*
Total Liabilities and Equity	*$527,500*	*$682,500*	*$778,500*	*$806,500*	*$721,500*

Note: The entries in the Balance Sheet that have changed compared to Table 5.2, due to the reduction in inventories by $20,000 per year, are shown by italics.

Table 5.7 ADJUSTED NET ASSET VALUATION METHOD

Steps	Procedure	Comments
1	Adjust the Balance Sheet to reflect the fair market value of assets.	Inventories are adjusted down by $20,000 in each year as shown in Table 5.6.
2	Determine the value of goodwill, if any.	No goodwill is assumed.
3	Subtract total liabilities from adjusted total assets to arrive at adjusted net assets.	This difference is noted on the balance sheet as total stockholders' equity; for 2009, stockholders' equity equals $121,500.
4	Adjust for transfer marketability as appropriate.	A 10% marketability discount is imputed to $121,500 to yield a fair market value of Business, Inc. of $109,350.

Using a 5–4–3–2–1 weighting scheme, the weighted average of the market value of adjusted tangible assets on the Adjusted Balance Sheet, or total stockholders' equity, is $194,767.[10] Assuming a risk-free rate at the end of 2009 of 6 percent, the expected return on the weighted average of the market value of adjusted tangible assets is $11,686.[11]

In this valuation illustration, excess earnings are defined to be the difference between the weighted average of adjusted future net earnings and the return expected on the weighted average of the market value of tangible assets. This difference is $55,194.[12] And, again assuming a 25 percent capitalization rate, the capitalized value of excess earnings is $220,776.[13]

The fair market value of adjusted tangible assets in 2009 is $121,500, as reported on the Adjusted Balance Sheet in Table 5.6. The sum of excess earnings and the fair market value of adjusted tangible assets is $342,276.[14] Adjusting only for marketability by 10 percent, the fair market value of Business, Inc. at the end of 2009 is thus $308,048.[15]

Table 5.8, which is based on Table 4.4, summarizes the above calculations.

Table 5.8 CAPITALIZATION OF EXCESS EARNINGS
VALUATION METHOD

Steps	Procedure	Comments
1	Calculate a weighted average of adjusted future earnings from the Income Statement.	This value is $66,880, as previously shown in Table 5.4.
2	Calculate a weighted average of the market value of adjusted tangible assets (stockholders' equity) from the Adjusted Balance Sheet.	This value is $194,767.

(Continued)

Table 5.8 CONTINUED

Steps	Procedure	Comments
3	Determine an expected return on the weighted average of the market value of adjusted tangible assets.	A risk-free rate at the end of 2009 is assumed for this example to be 6%. Thus, the expected return on the weighted average of the market value of adjusted tangible assets is $11,686.
4	Subtract the return expected on these adjusted tangible assets from the weighted average of adjusted future earnings to determine excess earnings.	Excess earnings are $55,194.
5	Capitalize excess earnings.	As in Table 5.4, a 25% capitalization rate is assumed. The capitalized value of excess earnings is $220,776.

(Continued)

Table 5.8 CONTINUED

Steps	Procedure	Comments
6	Add to the capitalized value of excess earnings the fair market value of current adjusted tangible assets and adjust the sum for marketability as appropriate.	The fair market value of adjusted tangible assets for 2009 is $121,500, as reported on the Adjusted Balance Sheet. The sum of the capitalized value of excess earnings and the fair market value of adjusted tangible assets is $342,276. Adjusting only for marketability by 10%, the fair market value of Business, Inc. is $308,048.

5.5 SUMMARY

We illustrated in this chapter simplified calculations for the four traditional valuation methods discussed in Chapter 4. Anticipating the discussion in the following chapters, each of these methods depends on the existence of revenue or tangible assets for the going concern. Revenue is not likely to exist in an entrepreneurial enterprise, but some tangible assets might. We begin to show the lack of applicability of these methods to an entrepreneurial enterprise in the following chapter.

NOTES

1 $66,880 = [($38,000 + $50,000) + (($46,000 + $50,000) × 2) + (($58,000 + $50,000) × 3) + (($50,000 - $14,000) × 4) + (($1,040 + $50,000) × 5)]/15.

2 $267,520 = ($66,880/0.25).

3 $240,768 = ($267,520 × 0.90).

4 Of course, the buyer and seller will arrive at their own estimates of fair market value. Should each have calculated a price-to-earnings ratio, there will likely be a difference of opinion as to what constitutes a comparable set of publicly traded companies.

5 $163,328 = ($51,040 × 3.2).

6 $146,995 = ($163,328 × 0.90).

7 $169,044 = ($146,995 × 1.15).

8 $71,724 = ($240,768 - $169,044).

9 $109,350 = ($121,500 × 0.90).

10 $194,767 = [$92,500 + ($209,500 × 2) + ($265,500 × 3) + ($251,500 × 4) + ($121,500 × 5)]/15.

11 $11,686 = ($194,767 × 0.06).

12 $55,194 = ($66,880 - $11,686).

13 $220,776 = ($55,194/0.25).

14 $342,276 = ($220,776 + $121,500).

15 $308,048 = ($342,276 × 0.90).

6

Alternative Approaches to the Valuations of Video, Inc.

In this chapter we illustrate, through example, the importance of understanding alternative and complementary technologies in the valuation process. As emphasized in the Introduction to this book, understanding alternative and complementary technologies is key to valuing an entrepreneurial enterprise. In this chapter and in Chapter 8 we illustrate that point through semi-realistic case studies. In fact, the case described in this chapter is conceptually based on a valuation that we conducted about a decade ago, hence the retrospective time nature of the description that follows.

Video, Inc. was a small, family-owned video rental business offered for sale in early 2002. The owner of the business wanted to retire within the next few years, but the timing of his retirement was not pressing. Thus, the business was valued as a going concern and not valued for the purpose of a liquidation sale.

The owner commissioned two valuations prior to putting the business up for sale. One valuation was commissioned from us, and a second valuation was commissioned from a hypothetical, yet experienced valuator at a prestigious and equally hypothetical local firm.[1] The owner simply wanted two different opinions from two different perspectives. Both of these valuations are described herein. For simplicity, as well as to keep the focus of this book less on specific numerical calculations and more on broader concepts, we assume that the actual and adjusted financial values in the Income Statements and Balance Sheets for Video, Inc. are the same as those for Business, Inc. in Chapter 5; we simply changed the dates to place the valuation in a relevant time period (as discussed below). What we are emphasizing in this chapter is the nexus between the assumptions that underlie the traditional valuation methods described in Chapters 4 and 5 and the realities of an entrepreneurial enterprise.

As background, Video, Inc. began renting videos in 1986. Previously, the family had operated a variety store in a small but growing town—Town, USA. However, as often happens, a large discount store opened along the town's bypass. To compete successfully with this new retailer, the owner of Video, Inc. had to alter the focus of his business from variety-related sales to something else. He needed to be entrepreneurial; that is, he needed to perceive a new direction for his business and then act on that perception. The video rental business was in its infancy at that time, and setting a new direction for the family business seemed right.

The remainder of this chapter is divided into three sections. Video, Inc.'s financial statements are presented in Section 6.1. The alternative valuations are described in Section 6.2. Section 6.3 concludes the chapter with a brief summary statement.

6.1 VIDEO, INC.'S FINANCIAL STATEMENTS

Video, Inc.'s Income Statement is in Table 6.1 and its Balance Sheet is in Table 6.2. The values in the Income Statement and Balance Sheet, for simplicity and pedagogical purposes, are the same as those for Business, Inc. (Tables 5.1 and 5.2). The Adjusted Income Statement and the Adjusted Balance Sheet from Tables 5.3 and 5.6 are below as Tables 6.3 and 6.4.

6.2 THE GOING-CONCERN VALUATION OF VIDEO, INC.

Were Video, Inc. being valued for liquidation purposes, we would have approached the valuation using an adjusted net asset valuation method based on the Adjusted Balance Sheet in Table 6.4. No doubt the valuator would have done the same thing, and both of us would likely have agreed on the value of $109,350 from Table 5.7—assuming that we agreed on the economic value of the business's inventory. However, Video, Inc. was to be valued as a going concern, and the present value of adjusted future net earnings valuation method seemed to both of us the most appropriate valuation method to use. Because the valuations occurred in early 2002, both of the valuations were referenced at the end of 2001 (the last full year of financial information).

The Valuator's Approach to Valuing Video, Inc.

The valuator's approach to this exercise followed the template in Table 5.4 for implementing a capitalized adjusted future net earnings valuation method. We refer to that template in Table 6.5.

More to the point, it has been our experience that very few individuals—regardless of their training or background—who are active in the valuation profession think in terms of alternative or complementary technologies when conducting valuations of technology-based businesses. At the time of the valuation, Video, Inc. was certainly a technology-based business. That said, this

Table 6.1 VIDEO, INC.: INCOME STATEMENT

	1997	1998	1999	2000	2001
Revenues:					
Video Rentals	$1,000,000	$1,265,000	$1,572,000	$1,803,000	$1,992,000
Operating Expenses:					
Cost of Goods	358,000	419,000	499,000	578,000	623,000
Owner's Compensation	150,000	175,000	209,000	299,000	355,000
Other Salaries	225,000	368,000	407,000	509,000	621,000
Payroll Taxes	40,000	46,000	52,000	69,000	83,000
Profit Sharing Plan	20,000	23,000	26,000	34,500	41,500
Misc. Supplies	10,000	12,000	15,000	18,000	21,000

Depreciation	20,000	25,000	30,000	35,000	40,000
Rent	75,000	85,000	95,000	105,000	115,000
Insurance	22,000	28,000	32,000	38,000	42,000
Other Expenses	42,000	38,000	149,000	131,500	49,460
Total Operating Expenses	$962,000	$1,219,000	$1,514,000	$1,817,000	$1,990,960
Net Earnings (Net Income)	$38,000	$46,000	$58,000	($14,000)	$1,040

Table 6.2 VIDEO, INC.: BALANCE SHEET

	1997	1998	1999	2000	2001
Current Assets:					
Cash	$ 25,000	$ 65,000	$105,000	$115,000	$ 75,000
Video Inventory	250,000	300,000	336,000	349,000	314,000
Prepaid Expenses	2,500	2,500	2,500	2,500	2,500
Total Current Assets	277,500	367,500	443,500	466,500	391,500
Property and Equipment:					
Leasehold Improvements	250,000	300,000	340,000	370,000	390,000
Office Furniture and Equipment	95,000	140,000	155,000	170,000	185,000
Accumulated Depreciation	(75,000)	(105,000)	(140,000)	(180,000)	(225,000)
Total Property and Equipment	270,000	335,000	355,000	360,000	350,000
Total Assets	$547,500	$702,500	$798,500	$826,500	$741,500

Current Liabilities:					
Accounts Payable	$200,000	$220,000	$242,000	$266,000	$293,000
Bank Loan	175,000	190,000	205,000	220,000	235,000
Accrued Salaries	15,000	16,000	17,000	18,000	19,000
Accrued Profit Sharing Contribution	30,000	32,000	34,000	36,000	38,000
Other Accrued Liabilities	15,000	15,000	15,000	15,000	15,000
Total Current Liabilities	435,000	473,000	513,000	555,000	600,000
Stockholders' Equity:					
Common Stock	10,000	10,000	10,000	10,000	10,000
Retained Earnings	102,500	219,500	275,500	261,500	131,500
Total Stockholders' Equity	112,500	229,500	285,500	271,500	141,500
Total Liabilities and Equity	$547,500	$702,500	$798,500	$826,500	$741,500

Table 6.3 VIDEO, INC.: ADJUSTED INCOME STATEMENT

	1997	1998	1999	2000	2001
Revenues:					
Video Rentals	$1,000,000	$1,265,000	$1,572,000	$1,803,000	$1,992,000
Operating Expenses:					
Cost of Goods	358,000	419,000	499,000	578,000	623,000
Owner's Compensation	100,000	125,000	159,000	249,000	305,000
Other Salaries	225,000	368,000	407,000	509,000	621,000
Payroll Taxes	40,000	46,000	52,000	69,000	83,000
Profit Sharing Plan	20,000	23,000	26,000	34,500	41,500
Misc. Supplies	10,000	12,000	15,000	18,000	21,000

Depreciation	20,000	25,000	30,000	35,000	40,000
Rent	75,000	85,000	95,000	105,000	115,000
Insurance	22,000	28,000	32,000	38,000	42,000
Other Expenses	42,000	38,000	149,000	131,500	49,460
Total Operating Expenses	$912,000	$1,169,000	$1,464,000	$1,767,000	$1,940,960
Adjusted Net Earnings (Adjusted Net Income)	$88,000	$96,000	$108,000	$36,000	$51,040

Table 6.4 VIDEO, INC.: ADJUSTED BALANCE SHEET

	1997	1998	1999	2000	2001
Current Assets:					
Cash	$ 25,000	$ 65,000	$105,000	$115,000	$ 75,000
Video Inventory	230,000	280,000	316,000	329,000	294,000
Prepaid Expenses	2,500	2,500	2,500	2,500	2,500
Total Current Assets	257,500	347,500	423,500	446,500	371,500
Property and Equipment:					
Leasehold Improvements	250,000	300,000	340,000	370,000	390,000
Office Furniture and Equipment	95,000	140,000	155,000	170,000	185,000
Accumulated Depreciation	(75,000)	(105,000)	(140,000)	(180,000)	(225,000)
Total Property and Equipment	270,000	335,000	355,000	360,000	350,000
Total Assets	$527,500	$682,500	$778,500	$806,500	$721,500

Current Liabilities:					
Accounts Payable	$293,000	$266,000	$242,000	$220,000	$200,000
Bank Loan	235,000	220,000	205,000	190,000	175,000
Accrued Salaries	19,000	18,000	17,000	16,000	15,000
Accrued Profit Sharing Contribution	38,000	36,000	34,000	32,000	30,000
Other Accrued Liabilities	15,000	15,000	15,000	15,000	15,000
Total Current Liabilities	600,000	555,000	513,000	473,000	435,000
Stockholders' Equity:					
Common Stock	10,000	10,000	10,000	10,000	10,000
Retained Earnings	111,500	241,500	255,500	199,500	82,500
Total Stockholders' Equity	121,500	251,500	265,500	209,500	92,500
Total Liabilities and Equity	$721,500	$806,500	$778,500	$682,500	$527,500

particular valuator did think in broader terms than many others with whom we have collaborated, but those terms were simply not broad enough.

The valuator offered two options for the fair market value of Video, Inc. as of the end of 2001 in the final (and hypothetical) valuation report. The first opinion was that the fair market value was $240,768, the same numerical value as for Business, Inc. that was discussed in Chapter 5. This similarity was intentional due to how the Income Statement in Table 6.1 and the Adjusted Income Statement in Table 6.3 were constructed. See Table 6.5 for the details of how this value was determined.

The valuator's second option did take into account complementary technology, albeit the wrong technology, in our opinion. Noted in the valuation report were statistics demonstrating that household ownership of video cassette recorders (VCRs)— certainly a complementary technology to VHS (Video Home System) and Betamax formatted video tapes—had increased dramatically since 1980. As shown in Table 6.6, which is an exhibit altered from the valuator's final valuation report, 96 million households had a VCR by the end of 2001, up from 63 million in 1990. This represented 86.2 percent of households, up from 68.6 percent in 1990. Between 1980 and 2001, VCRs in households had increased, on average, by 4.5 million per year. Between 1990 and 2001, VCRs in households had increased by 3 million per year, and sales had increased by 4.8 percent per year over the same period of time. Similarly, the percentage of households with VCRs had increased by 4.1 percent and 1.6 percent between 1980 and 2001 and 1990 and 2001, respectively. Thus, the valuator concluded that the video rental business was vibrant over this period of time and would likely remain that way for the foreseeable future. The error the valuator made was to forecast

Table 6.5 VALUATOR'S PRESENT VALUE OF ADJUSTED FUTURE NET EARNINGS VALUATION OF VIDEO, INC.

Steps	Procedure	Comments
1	Determine the expected life of the business—a limited life of n years or an indefinite life.	In this example, an infinite life of the business is assumed.
2	Estimate an appropriate discount rate, r.	Building on a risk free rate of 6% and taking into account competitive risk, regulatory risk, cost risk, marketability risk, and financial risk, the appropriate discount rate is 25%.
3	Normalize the Income Statement.	Owner's compensation is adjusted by $50,000 per year. This adjustment is tantamount to increasing net earnings on the Income Statement by $50,000 per year. No other adjustments are made to the Income Statement.

(Continued)

Table 6.5 (Continued)

Steps	Procedure	Comments
4	Calculate a weighted average of adjusted net earnings, assuming that a weighted average of adjusted net earnings is appropriate.	Using a 5–4–3–2–1 weighting scheme, the weighted average of adjusted net earnings is $66,880.
5	Calculate the present value of the weighted average of adjusted net earnings using either the limited life present value equation (4.1), to which a residual value for the business must then be added, or the capitalization equation (4.2).	Based on a discount rate of 25%, the present value of the weighted average of adjusted net earnings is $267,520.
6	Adjust for marketability as appropriate.	No ownership control adjustment is necessary because the entire business is being valued for sale, but a 10% marketability discount is appropriate. Thus, the fair market value of Video, Inc. as of the end of 2001 is $240,768.

the future from this past trend and thus assume that the video rental business would continue of the growth of the previous decade.[2]

The valuator's second estimate of the value of Video, Inc. as of the end of 2001 was based on a variation of equation (4.2) that took into account the presumed future growth of the video rental business. In Chapter 4, we discussed equation (4.2) and its implicit assumptions of zero future growth in AFE with reference to a capitalized value of a business. Specifically:

$$PV = \$AFE / r \qquad (6.1)$$

The valuator altered equation (4.2) to account for continued growth in the VCR market in the future. In fact, by choosing a capitalization approach, the valuator was explicitly assuming that this historical growth would last indefinitely.

Implicit in our earlier formulation of either equation (4.2) or (6.1) is that the value of adjusted future net earnings or, more likely, the weighted average of adjusted future net earnings remains constant for the indefinite future. To impute a growth factor to the value of the weighted average of adjusted future net earnings of $66,880 from Table 6.5, the valuator multiplied it by 4.8 percent (see Table 6.6; this will be the value for g below) or by 1.048 to obtain what might be called a growth-adjusted value of the weighted average of adjusted future net earnings; this value is $70,090.[3] In other words, the valuator adjusted equation (6.1) to impute a growth rate, g, to the calculation of the present value of adjusted future earnings as:

$$PV = \left(\$AFE \times \left(1 + g\right)\right) / r \qquad (6.2)$$

Table 6.6 UTILIZATION OF VIDEO CASSETTE RECORDERS
BY U.S. HOUSEHOLDS

Year	VCR Sales (millions)	% Households
1980	1	1.1
1990	63	68.6
1996	77	81.0
1998	83	84.6
1999	86	84.6
2000	88	85.1
2001	96	86.2
Average Increase per Year		
1980–2001	4.5 million per year	4.1% per year
1990–2001	3.0 million or 4.8% per year	1.6% per year

Source: U.S. Census Bureau, *Statistical Abstract of the United States* (2009).

Capitalizing the growth-adjusted value of the weighted average of adjusted future net earnings from equation (6.2) ($70,090) using a 25 percent discount rate, r, yields a non-marketability adjusted fair market value for Video, Inc. of $280,360.[4] And finally, adjusting by a 10 percent marketability factor, the valuator concluded that a second estimate of the fair market value of the company as of the end of 2001 was $252,324.[5]

Thus, the valuator offered two estimates of the fair market value of Video, Inc. as of the end of 2001. The first value was $240,768 from Table 6.5 and the second value was $252,324 from equation (6.2).[6]

Our Approach to Valuating Video, Inc.

As we stated in the Introduction, the thrust of our message is simple; when valuing an entrepreneurial enterprise—a technology-based entrepreneurial enterprise in particular—the key is to understand the availability of alternative or complementary technologies rather than the existence of substitutable products (which, by our definition of an entrepreneurial enterprise, would not exist). Regarding Video, Inc., there were no other movie formats in 2002 that were a substitute for either VHS- or Betamax-formatted videos, and there were no other locations or vacancies in downtown Town, USA in which another business could currently or in the foreseeable future locate and effectively compete. But, there was a replacement technology on the horizon which would soon make the movie rental business (and the VCR trends in Table 6.6) obsolete, namely optical fiber technology.

To set the stage for our approach, we did some research on optical communications as a complementary technology. We learned that voice transmission using light is not a new technology. As early as 1880, Alexander Graham Bell reported such transmission.[7] Many inventors in the early 1900s also experimented with this technology, but they had limited success. There were two problems with the development and early use of optical communications: the lack of a suitable light source and the lack of a suitable transmission medium.

There are three critical elements to an optical fiber system: a transmitter to convert electrical impulses into light impulses (i.e., electrons into photons), a transmission medium (i.e., the optical fiber), and a receiver to recode the light impulses into electrical impulses (i.e., photodiodes early on). In the late 1950s, spurred by research at Bell Laboratories, the major technological breakthrough associated with optical communication systems occurred in the form of Light Amplification by Stimulated Emission of Radiation, or the laser. The only missing element for optical communications was a suitable transmission medium.

Although the American Optical Company and the Standard Telecommunications Laboratories in the United Kingdom were early developers of optical fiber, neither was able to overcome the critical technical barrier to commercialization: signal loss. What was needed was a technological breakthrough in the design of the fiber core, namely a glass with minimal absorption of light pulses due to impurities. In the mid-1970s, Corning developed a core with an acceptable attenuation rate.

Corning began to operate its first factory to produce optical fiber in 1979, and in 1980 AT&T announced their intention to build a 611-mile fiberoptic network between Cambridge, Massachusetts and Washington, D.C. They did, and optical fiber communications became—both in concept and fact—a reality.

However, very few technologies can be successfully commercialized and achieve significant market penetration without the availability and use of critical technology infrastructure. Such infrastructure includes measurement and test methods, databases used in R&D and process control, and generic models of scientific and engineering phenomena. As with more conventional economic infrastructure, technology infrastructure is used by all market participants more or less equally, to leverage productivity and quality and to lower transaction costs.

The National Institute of Standards and Technology (NIST) had been supportive of the optical fiber industry since its inception. NIST personnel were involved in providing basic measurement technology, evaluating test procedures through interlaboratory comparisons, and offering technical assistance by writing significant fiber-optic test procedures (FOTPs) in cooperation with the Electronic Industries Alliance (EIA). These FOTPs are listed in Table 6.7, along with the fiber characteristics to which each is relevant.[8]

In early 2002, when we were asked to perform our valuation of Video, Inc., it was clear that once FOTP-176 and FOTP-177 were promulgated—and they definitely would be because all interlaboratory comparisons had previously been completed—all relevant standards would be in place for the rapid growth and use of optical fiber communications. What this meant for the video rental business in general and for Video, Inc. in particular was that not only would video-on-demand through in-home cable replace VCR technology but also previous trends in the market penetration and use of attendant technologies, such as VCRs, would not be meaningful predictors of future video rentals. Thus, from a valuation perspective, our knowledge of this complementary technology—complementary to video-on-demand rather than to VCR rentals—prompted us to value Video, Inc. not on the valuator's assumption of an indefinite life but rather on our assumption of, say, a ten-year maximum horizon with no growth in sales.

Table 6.7 EIA FIBER-OPTIC TEST PROCEDURES (FOTPs)

FOTP[1]	Description	Characteristic[2]
FOTP-29	Refractive Index Profile Transverse Interference Method (issued August 1981)	Core diameter, numerical aperture
FOTP-30	Frequency Domain Measurement of Multi-Mode Optical Fiber Information Transmission Capacity (issued September 1982)	Bandwidth
FOTP-43	Output Near-Field Radiation Pattern Measurement of Optical Waveguide Fibers (issued December 1984)	Core diameter
FOTP-44	Refractive Index Profile, Refracted Ray Method (issued January 1984)	Core diameter, numerical aperture
FOTP-46	Spectral Attenuation Measurement for Long-Length, Graded-Index Optical Fibers (issued May 1983)	Attenuation
FOTP-47	Output Far-Field Radiation Pattern Measurement (issued September 1983)	Numerical aperture

FOTP-50	Light-Launch Conditions for Long-Length, Graded-Index Optical Fiber Spectral Attenuation Measurements (issued February 1983)	
FOTP-51	Pulse Distortion Measurement of Multi-Mode Glass Optical Fiber Information Transmission Capacity (issued September 1983)	Bandwidth
FOTP-54	Mode Scrambler Launch Requirements for Information Transmission Capacity Measurements (issued September 1982)	Bandwidth
FOTP-58	Core Diameter Measurement of Graded-Index Optical Fibers (issued December 1984)	Core diameter
FOTP-78	Spectral Attenuation Cut-Back Measurement for Single-Mode Optical Fibers (issued February 1987)	Attenuation
FOTP-80	Cut-Off Wavelength of Uncabled Single-Model Fiber by Transmitted Power (issued October 1988)	Cut-off wavelength
FOTP-95	Absolute Optical Power Test for Optical Fibers and Cables (issued June 1986)	

(Continued)

Table 6.7 (CONTINUED)

FOTP[1]	Description	Characteristic[2]
FOTP-164	Single-Mode Fiber, Measurement of Mode Field Diameter by Far-Field Scanning (issued December 1986)	Mode-field diameter
FOTP-165	Single-Mode Fiber, Measurement of Mode-field diameter by Near-Field Scanning (issued December 1986)	Mode-field diameter
FOTP-166	Single-Mode Fiber, Measurement of Mode-field diameter by Transverse Offset (issued December 1986)	Mode-field diameter
FOTP-167	Mode-field Diameter Measurement Variable Aperture Method in the Far Field (issued July 1987)	Mode-field diameter
FOTP-168	Chromatic Dispersion Measurement of Multi-Mode Graded-Index and Single-Model Optical Fibers by Spectral Group Delay Measurement in the Time Domain (issued July 1987)	Chromatic dispersion

FOTP-169	Chromatic Dispersion Measurement of Single-Mode Optical Fibers by Phase-Shift Method (issued August 1988)	Chromatic dispersion
FOTP-175	Chromatic Dispersion, Differential Phase Shift (issued November 1989)	Chromatic dispersion
FOTP-176	Measurement Method for Optical Fiber Geometry by Automated Grey-Scale Analysis (issued May 2003)	Geometry
FOTP-177	Numerical Aperture Measurement of Graded-Index Optical Fibers (issued August 2003)	Numerical aperture

Notes:

[1] A higher numbered FOTP could be issued in an earlier year than a lower numbered one because the evaluation period was longer. FOTPs are numbered when the evaluation period begins.

[2] Some FOTPs do not refer to characteristics of the optical fiber but to measurement methods or to characteristics of the light emitting source launching conditions. Thus, that cell in the table is blank.

Source: Link (1992).

Table 6.8 outlines our analysis. Basically, we applied the formula for the present value of adjusted future net earnings from equation (4.1) using a ten-year life for the business, a 1–1 weighting scheme for adjusted future net earnings of $43,520, and a 35 percent discount rate:[9]

$$PV = \left[\$43,250/(1+0.35)^1 \right] + \ldots + \left[\$43,450/(1+0.35)^{10} \right] \quad (6.3)$$

Because of the expected obsolescence of VHS and the already-declining use of Betamax formatting and the attendant VCR technology in favor of video-on-demand, only the last two years of adjusted future net earnings from Table 6.3 were considered for the valuation. The values for these last two years were weighted equally, thus the 1–1 weighting scheme is equivalent to calculating a simple mathematical mean of adjusted future net earnings for 2000 and 2001. Similarly, a discount rate of 35 percent was used in the present value calculation from equation (6.3). The additional ten percentage points (see Table 6.8) were added because of any future market risk associated with consumer adoption of video-on-demand technology.

The resulting present value from equation (6.3) is $118,159. Imputing a 10 percent marketability discount, it was our opinion that the fair market value of Video, Inc. at the end of 2001 was $106,343.[10]

This value is slightly less than the liquidation value of the company of $109,350. We thus recommended in our final valuation report that the owner of Video, Inc. liquidate his net assets rather than remain in what was inevitably a declining growth industry. Of course, the fair market value of a going concern is in theory performed under the assumption that both parties are fully informed. However, in reality, some are indeed, to re-quote Machlup, more

Table 6.8 OUR PRESENT VALUE OF ADJUSTED FUTURE NET EARNINGS VALUATION OF VIDEO, INC.

Steps	Procedure	Comments
1	Determine the expected life of the business—a limited life of n years or an indefinite life.	We assumed a 10-year life for the business with $0 residual value after that time.
2	Estimate an appropriate discount rate, r.	We used a 35% discount rate, although a higher rate could have been justified because overall business risk had increased in light of the inevitability of video-on-demand, given that all FOTPs would be in place within approximately 1 year.
3	Normalize the Income Statement.	Owner's compensation is adjusted by $50,000 per year. This adjustment is tantamount to increasing net earnings on the Income Statement by $50,000 per year. No other adjustments are made to the Income Statement.

(Continued)

Table 6.8 (CONTINUED)

Steps	Procedure	Comments
4	Calculate a weighted average of adjusted net earnings assuming that a weighted average of adjusted net earnings is appropriate.	A 1–1 weighting scheme was used because there was sufficient information to suggest that the most recent 2-year period of sales was the period most indicative of future year's sales. Thus, in effect a 1–1 weighting scheme was used, that is, the mean of adjusted future net earnings was used: $43,520.
5	Calculate the present value of the weighted average of adjusted net earnings using either the limited life present value equation (4.1), to which a residual value for the business must then be added, or the capitalization equation (4.2).	Based on a discount rate of 35%, the present value of the unweighted average of adjusted future net earnings is $118,159.
6	Adjust marketability as appropriate.	No ownership control adjustment is needed because the entire business is being valued for sale, but a 10% marketability discount is appropriate. Thus, the fair market value of Video, Inc. at of the end of 2001 is $106,343.

alert and quick minded and some might perceive what "normal people of lesser alertness and perceptiveness would fail to notice" (1980, p. 179).

6.3 SUMMARY

This chapter and Chapter 8 are the punch-line chapters in this book. They emphasize through example the importance of accounting for complementary technologies when valuing an entrepreneurial enterprise. Although the example in this chapter is relevant to a technology-based company, the example in Chapter 8 goes one step further by addressing the issue of zero revenues when conducting a valuation of an entrepreneurial enterprise.

NOTES

1 We have taken liberties with regard to the practitioner's valuation of the business in order to emphasize the theme of this book. The valuator is simply a straw man.

2 Retrospectively, the percentage of households with VCRs grew to 91.5% by 2003; then it began to decline. 2006 was the last year that these data were reported by the U.S. Census Bureau (2009), and the percentage was 88.6. However, that percentage does not imply that the VCRs were in fact being used.

3 $70,090 = ($66,880 \times 1.048)$.

4 $280,360 = ($70,090/0.25)$.

5 $252,324 = ($280,360 \times 0.90)$.

6 The second value is 4.8% larger than the first value. Any value calculated from equation (6.2) will be $(1 + g)$ greater than a value calculated from equation (6.1).

7 This discussion about optical fiber technology is based on Link (1992).

8 NIST has a responsibility to enhance the competitiveness of American industry while maintaining its traditional function as lead national laboratory for providing the measurement, calibrations, and quality assurance techniques

which underpin U.S. commerce, technological progress, improved product reliability and manufacturing processes, and public safety. More specifically, NIST's responsibility is to prepare, certify, and sell standard reference materials for use in ensuring the accuracy of chemical analyses and measurements of physical and other properties of materials.

An industry standard is a set of specifications to which all elements of products, processes, formats, or procedures under its jurisdiction must conform. The process of standardization is the pursuit of this conformity, with the objective of increasing the efficiency of economic activity. The complexity of modern technology, especially its system characteristics, has led to an increase in the number and variety of standards that affect a single industry or market. Standards affect the R&D, production, and market penetration stages of economic activity. Therefore, they have a significant collective effect on innovation, productivity, and market structure.

In one sense, standardization is a form rather than a type of infrastructure because it represents a codification of an element of an industry's technology or simply information relevant to the conduct of economic activity. The process of standardization is important because the selection of one of several available forms of a technology element as the standard has potentially important economic effects. While economics is increasingly concerned with the proliferation and pervasiveness of standards in many new high-technology industries, the economic roles of standards are unfortunately poorly understood.

Standards can be grouped into two basic categories: product-element standards, and non-product-element standards. This distinction is important because the economic role of each type is different. Product-element standards typically involve one of the key attributes or elements of a product as opposed to the entire product. In most cases, market dynamics determine product-element standards. Alternative technologies compete intensely until a dominant version gains sufficient market share to become the single de facto standard. Market control by one firm can truncate this competitive process. Conversely, non-product-element standards tend to be competitively neutral within the context of an industry. This type of standard can impact an entire industry's efficiency and its overall market penetration rate.

Industry organizations often set non-product-element standards using consensus processes. The technical bases (infrastructure technologies or infratechnologies) for these standards have a large public good content. Examples include measurement and test methods, interface standards, and standard reference materials.

From both the positions of a strategically focused firm, as well as of a public policymaker, standardization is not an all-or-nothing proposition. In complementary system technologies—such as distributed data processing, telecommunications, or factory automation—standardization typically proceeds in an evolutionary manner in lockstep with the evolution of the technology. Complete standardization too early in the technology's life cycle can constrain innovation.

The overall economic value of a standard is determined by its functionality (i.e., interaction with other standards at the systems level) and the cost of implementation (i.e., compliance costs). Standards should be competitively neutral, which means adaptable to alternative applications of a generic technology over that technology's life cycle.

9 $43,520 = ((($50,000 - $14,000) + $51,040)/2).

10 $106,343 = ($118,159 × 0.90).

Toward a Methodology for Valuing an Entrepreneurial Enterprise

This chapter sets the stage for the following chapter in which we present a more complete valuation of an entrepreneurial enterprise than we did in the simple and somewhat structured—although based on an actual experience—example in Chapter 6. Recall that the Video, Inc. example in Chapter 6 was intended to be a stepping stone to this chapter and, more specifically, to Chapter 8. Through the Video, Inc. example, the assumption of an indefinite life for the going-concern business was shown to be inappropriate in light of the impending competing technology and its complementary standards.

In this chapter, we reproduce in Tables 7.1 through 7.4 the step-by-step valuation tables from Chapter 4 for each of the four traditional valuation methods and thereby move toward a methodology for valuing an entrepreneurial enterprise.[1] Here, within each table, we comment on the lack of necessary information for the valuation of an entrepreneurial enterprise. Thus, these annotated tables not only become the explanatory text for this chapter, but also they document the theme of this book.

Table 7.1 PRESENT VALUE OF ADJUSTED FUTURE NET
EARNINGS VALUATION METHOD

Steps	Procedure	Comments about Applicability for an Entrepreneurial Enterprise
1	Determine the expected life of the business—a limited life of n years or an indefinite life.	Given the nature of an entrepreneurial enterprise and its entrepreneur, it is impossible to determine the life of the enterprise. To do so would be, to paraphrase Machlup from Chapter 1, to anticipate when the next alert and quick-minded person would—by keeping his or her eyes and ears open for new facts and theories, discoveries and opportunities—perceive a new opportunity.
2	Estimate an appropriate discount rate, r.	Because the discount rate reflects the resource and market risk of the enterprise, and because there are no comparables, r cannot be estimated.
3	Normalize the Income Statement.	By definition, there are no revenues on the enterprise's Income Statement. Normalizing it for, say, owner's compensation could be done, but it would have no useful value.

(Continued)

Table 7.1 CONTINUED

Steps	Procedure	Comments about Applicability for an Entrepreneurial Enterprise
4	Calculate a weighted average of adjusted future net earnings assuming that a weighted average of adjusted future net earnings is appropriate.	There are no net earnings to weight.
5	Calculate the present value of the weighted average of adjusted future net earnings using either the limited life present value equation (4.1), to which a residual value for the business must then be added, or the capitalization equation (4.2).	Absent net earnings, no present value can be calculated.
6	Adjust for marketability as appropriate.	Absent a present value estimate, a marketability adjustment is meaningless.

Table 7.2 PRICE-TO-EARNINGS RATIO VALUATION METHOD

Steps	Procedure	Comments about Applicability for an Entrepreneurial Enterprise
1	Identify a publicly traded company or set of publicly traded companies and calculate a price-to-earnings ratio, $(P/E)_{comparable}$.	By definition of an entrepreneurial enterprise, there are no publicly traded companies that are comparable.
2	Normalize the income statement to determine $AFE_{business}$.	By definition, there are no revenues on the enterprise's Income Statement. Normalizing it for, say, owner's compensation could be done, but it would have no useful value.
3	Multiply the above two values and then adjust the product by a publicly traded marketability discount.	This is a moot step absent the above information.
4	Adjust by an ownership premium.	This too is a moot step.

Table 7.3 ADJUSTED NET ASSET VALUATION METHOD

Steps	Procedure	Comments about Applicability for an Entrepreneurial Enterprise
1	Adjust the Balance Sheet to reflect the fair market value of assets.	An entrepreneurial enterprise will have a Balance Sheet even in the absence of revenues, and whatever assets it has will have a market value. However, the relevant assets of the enterprise are cognitive; that is, they are the vision of the entrepreneur and that will not show up on the Balance Sheet.
2	Determine the value of goodwill, if any.	There is no quantifiable or marketable goodwill in an entrepreneurial enterprise.
3	Subtract total liabilities from adjusted total assets to arrive at adjusted net assets.	Net assets can be calculated, but for the reasons stated in step 1, net assets from the Balance Sheet will understate the true asset value of the enterprise.
4	Adjust for transfer marketability as appropriate.	It would be guess work, we think, to estimate if there is a buyer much less when he or she might come forward.

Table 7.4 CAPITALIZATION OF EXCESS EARNINGS
VALUATION METHOD

Steps	Procedure	Comments about Applicability for an Entrepreneurial Enterprise
1	Calculate a weighted average of adjusted future net earnings from the Income Statement.	There are no adjusted future net earnings to weight.
2	Calculate a weighted average of the market value of tangible assets (stockholders' equity) from the Balance Sheet.	This step can be done, subject to the caveats discussed with reference to the adjustments to the Balance Sheet in Table 7.3.
3	Determine an expected return on the weighted average of the market value of tangible assets.	Subject to the same caveats as in step 2, a risk-free market rate of return would be applicable.
4	Subtract the return expected on these tangible assets from the weighted average of adjusted future net earnings to determine excess earnings.	This step cannot be done because there are not adjusted future net earnings.

(Continued)

Table 7.4 CONTINUED

Steps	Procedure	Comments about Applicability for an Entrepreneurial Enterprise
5	Capitalize excess earnings.	Because there are no excess earnings, there is no value to capitalize.
6	Add to the capitalized value of excess earnings the fair market value of current tangible assets and adjust the sum for ownership control and marketability.	This step cannot be done because of missing information.

Our conclusion from these tables, taken either individually or as a group, is that none of the four traditional and widely accepted valuation methods is applicable to an entrepreneurial enterprise. In fact, information relevant to a valuation will likely only be available to permit one to arrive at a numerical calculation using the adjusted net asset valuation method, but that method is, as we have discussed, most applicable for determining a liquidation value rather than a going-concern value. If nothing else, an entrepreneur and his or her entrepreneurial enterprise is planning to be a going concern.[2]

NOTES

1   It is important to emphasize the difference between the terms *methodology* and *method*. The terms are often used interchangeably, although it is incorrect to do so. A *methodology* is the theoretical foundation or practices within a discipline that determine or guide how to engage in an inquiry; a *method* is a tool or technique used to implement the inquiry.
2   Recall in the Video, Inc. example in Chapter 6 that we calculated both a liquidation value and a going-concern value using the present value of expected future net earnings with a ten-year life method. In that case, the liquidation value was greater than the going-concern value, primarily due to the assumption of a ten-year life.

Valuation of Metal Brothers, Inc.

This chapter illustrates the valuation of a technology-based entrepreneurial enterprise, Metal Brothers, Inc., that is new and that has $0 revenues during the year that it has been operating. Fundamental to the valuation of this enterprise is the availability of complementary technologies from which a valuator can forecast future revenues.[1]

The remainder of this chapter is divided into four sections. Important background information, which sets the stage for the calculation exercise, is in Section 8.1. The financial statements for Metal Brothers, Inc. are in Section 8.2. The valuation calculations are in Section 8.3. The chapter concludes with a brief summary statement in Section 8.4.

8.1 BACKGROUND INFORMATION

The Metal brothers received a patent from the U.S. Patent and Trademark Office in December 2009 for a process of making a new aluminum alloy stronger than any existing material currently used in passenger cars and lightweight trucks. This process could allow more aluminum to be used in the construction of a vehicle's frame in place of steel, at a price that is cost-effective for automobile manufacturers. On January 1, 2010, the brothers founded Metal Brothers, Inc.

Since 2003, they had been researching and experimenting on a part-time basis with processes for making various aluminum alloys. They filed for their patent in mid-2007 in anticipation of President George W. Bush signing the Energy Independence and Security Act of 2007 on December 19 (Public Law 110–140).[2]

As background, Corporate Average Fuel Economy (CAFÉ) standards were established by the U.S. Energy Policy and Conservation Act of 1975 (Public Law 94–163). As shown in Tables 8.1 and 8.2, CAFÉ standards in the United Stated have slowly increased. The goal of increasing fuel efficiency to 35 miles per gallon by the end of 2020 as required by the Energy Independence and Security Act of 2007 represented a major, and some might even say ambitious, step toward energy conservation and air pollution control. This Act, albeit viewed by many as being in society's best interest, represented a major financial and technological challenge to U.S. automobile manufacturers that had to meet this standard.[3]

One way to increase fuel efficiency is to make an automobile lighter in weight. According to an Oak Ridge National Laboratory report:

> With…an average fuel economy of at least 35 mpg, the pressure to lightweight vehicles is stronger than ever before. The next few years will see considerable lightweighting across the automotive industry. Vehicle lightweighting represents one of several design approaches automakers are currently evaluating to improve fuel economy. Lightweighting is typically accomplished by downsizing, integrating parts and functions, *substituting materials* [emphasis added], or by combining these methods.
>
> (Das 2009, p.1)

Table 8.1 CAFÉ STANDARDS FOR PASSENGER CARS

Model Year	MPG	Model Year	MPG
1978	18.0	1995	27.5
1979	19.0	1996	27.5
1980	20.0	1997	27.5
1981	22.0	1998	27.5
1982	24.0	1999	27.5
1983	26.0	2000	27.5
1984	27.0	2001	27.5
1985	27.5	2002	27.5
1986	26.0	2003	27.5
1987	26.0	2004	27.5
1988	26.0	2005	27.5
1989	26.5	2006	27.5
1990	27.5	2007	27.5
1991	27.5	2008	27.5
1992	27.5	2009	27.5
1993	27.5	2010	27.5
1994	27.5		

Source: U.S. Department of Energy (2010).

Table 8.2 CAFÉ STANDARDS FOR LIGHTWEIGHT TRUCKS

Model Year	MPG	Model Year	MPG
1978	–[a]	1995	20.6
1979	–[a]	1996	20.7
1980	–[a]	1997	20.7
1981	–[a]	1998	20.7
1982	17.5	1999	20.7
1983	19.0	2000	20.7
1984	20.0	2001	20.7
1985	19.5	2002	20.7
1986	20.0	2003	20.7
1987	20.5	2004	20.7
1988	20.5	2005	21.0
1989	20.5	2006	21.6
1990	20.0	2007	22.2
1991	20.2	2008	22.5
1992	20.2	2009	23.1
1993	20.4	2010	23.5
1994	20.5		

Notes: [a] No combined CAFÉ standards for two-wheel and four-wheel drive trucks are available.
Source: U.S. Department of Energy (2010).

The Metal brothers, aware of this trend, believed that they were in a unique position to sell their newly created company and its intellectual property to an automobile manufacturer or to one of its materials suppliers.[4] However, they needed an independent valuation of their company.

8.2 FINANCIAL STATEMENTS FOR METAL BROTHERS, INC.

The company's Income Statement is in Table 8.3. It has $0 revenues for 2010. The Metal brothers were drawing on personal savings to finance this venture, and thus owner's compensation was $0 in 2010. Part of their initial business plan was to sell the business in 2011 to an automobile manufacturer or to one of its materials suppliers, but they did not know how to value their entrepreneurial enterprise. The valuator they retained pointed out some bad news and some good news.

First, the bad news. The valuator, who had some prior experience in the automobile industry broadly defined, was aware that lighter vehicles may not be as safe as heavier vehicles. Thus, automobile manufacturers might not be interested in purchasing Metal Brothers, Inc. until new safety devices were in place, regardless of the potential impact on fuel efficiency.

The valuator showed the Metal brothers a recent U.S. Department of Transportation report (2003) that concluded that, in most instances, driver and passenger fatalities would increase as automobile weight decreased. For example, consider a passenger car weighing 2,950 pounds or more (and less than 6,000 pounds by definition of a passenger car) that hits a fixed object (see Table 8.4). In that situation, a 100-pound reduction in the weight of the passenger car will

Table 8.3 INCOME STATEMENT FOR METAL BROTHERS, INC

	2010
Revenues:	
Patent Licensing Fees	$0
Operating Expenses:	
Cost of Goods	36,000
Owner's Compensation	0
Other Salaries	12,000
Payroll Taxes	1,250
Profit Sharing Plan	0
Misc. Supplies	2,000
Depreciation	800
Rent	24,000
Insurance	9,000
Other Expenses	3,000
Total Operating Expenses	$88,050
Net Earnings (Net Income)	($88,050)

Table 8.4 FATALITY INCREASE PER 100-POUND WEIGHT REDUCTION (INTERVAL ESTIMATE IN %)

Crash Category	Cars < 2,950 lbs.	Cars ≥ 2,950 lbs.	Light Trucks < 3,870 lbs.	Light Trucks ≥ 3,870 lbs.
Principle rollover	0.87 to 7.55	2.40 to 7.00	0.64 to 4.30	0.81 to 3.94
Fixed object	0.25 to 4.45	0.63 to 2.71	1.71 to 4.97	1.41 to 4.34
Ped/bike/motorcycle	0.22 to 5.00	−1.83 to 0.59	−1.26 to 2.38	−1.56 to 1.45
Heavy truck	2.50 to 7.68	0.67 to 3.45	3.10 to 7.36	−1.61 to 2.48
Car < 2,950 lbs.	−0.72 to 7.16	0.70 to 2.48	–	–
Car ≥ 2,950 lbs.	−0.36 to 3.58	1.40 to 4.96	–	–
Light truck	2.85 to 6.67	1.74 to 3.55	–	–

Car	—	—	−0.92 to 1.82	−1.79 to 0.06
Light truck < 3,870 lbs.	—	—	1.92 to 9.32	−3.20 to −0.17
Light truck ≥ 3,870 lbs.	—	—	0.96 to 4.66	−6.40 to −0.34
Overall	1.66 to 5.25	1.19 to 2.78	0.73 to 3.67	−1.06 to 1.64

Source: U.S. Department of Transportation (2003).

result in an increase in driver or passenger fatalities of between 0.63 and 2.71 percent. In this particular situation, the annual net increase in fatalities associated with the reduction in vehicle weight would be between 18 and 76 persons.

The good news was that the company could be valued in a systematic and defensible way for possible sale regardless of the fact that it earned $0 revenues in 2010. The reason the valuator was able to do this was that there were complementary technologies on the horizon that would offset the likelihood of an increase in fatalities from a lighter vehicle, thus increasing the demand for Metal Brothers, Inc. and its patented technology. The complementary technologies under consideration were improved safety devices that, all else held constant, would lessen the likelihood of a vehicle accident and thus a vehicle fatality.

Several companies had received research grants from the U.S. Department of Energy in 2007 and 2008 to develop new safety devices that could be installed on vehicles during the assembly stage of manufacturing. These technologies included, among other things, sensor-based adaptive cruise controls that would automatically adjust the speed of the vehicle when it approached an object (animate or inanimate) in front. Video technology could be installed on an automobile that would sense lane lines and markings and thus alert the driver, through sound and a self-correcting mechanism, if the vehicle was unintentionally swerving. Software-based technology customized to the driver of the vehicle could detect if the driver was losing control of the vehicle (e.g., as a result of falling asleep) and trigger the application of the brakes to slow the vehicle. Coupled with the other technologies, this software could keep the vehicle within its lane and away from objects in front. Because these complementary technologies were publicly funded, annual progress reports from the companies that developed them were available in the public domain. Thus, the valuator knew that these technologies could be commercialized in late 2012 and installed on new vehicles beginning in 2014.

Based on this knowledge and on the underlying trends in the complementary technologies, the valuator was able to forecast critical valuation information, namely future revenues, and thus future net earnings for the company. These forecasts were based on informed opinions regarding the availability of new safety devices in late 2012, as well as on the expected number of new domestic car sales in future years.

Tables 8.5 and 8.6 show new car and light-truck sales from 1978 through 2010. Based on a visual inspection of the data, the trend for both has been downward overtime, primarily due to increased imports and most recently to an overall economic slowdown. In 2009, just over 66 percent of new car sales were from a domestic manufacturer and just over 82 percent of new lightweight trucks were from a domestic manufacturer.[5]

Using these percentages and estimating future new car and light-truck sales, the valuator estimated the company's revenues from 2011 through 2016, as shown in the Adjusted Income Statement in Table 8.7.

8.3 PRESENT VALUE OF ADJUSTED FUTURE NET EARNINGS

Table 8.8 reproduces (from Table 4.1) the steps involved in the calculation of the present value of adjusted future net earnings. Thus:

- The life of the Metal brother's patent is assumed to be six years, that is, from 2011 through 2016.

Table 8.5 NEW RETAIL VEHICLE SALES OF CARS
IN THE UNITED STATES (1,000)

Model Year	Cars	Model Year	Cars
1978	11,314	1995	8,635
1979	10,673	1996	8,526
1980	8,949	1997	8,272
1981	8,489	1998	8,142
1982	7,956	1999	8,698
1983	9,148	2000	8,847
1984	10,324	2001	8,423
1985	10,979	2002	8,103
1986	11,404	2003	7,610
1987	10,192	2004	7,545
1988	10,547	2005	7,720
1989	9,779	2006	7,821
1990	9,303	2007	7,618
1991	8,189	2008	6,813
1992	8,213	2009	5,456
1993	8,518	2010	5,998 est.
1994	8,991		

Sources: U.S. Department of Energy (2010).

Table 8.6 NEW RETAIL SALES OF LIGHT TRUCKS IN THE UNITED STATES (1,000)

Model Year	Light Trucks	Model Year	Light Trucks
1978	3,808	1995	6,053
1979	3,311	1996	6,519
1980	2,440	1997	6,797
1981	2,189	1998	7,299
1982	2,479	1999	8,073
1983	2,984	2000	8,387
1984	3,863	2001	8,700
1985	4,458	2002	8,713
1986	4,594	2003	8,938
1987	4,610	2004	9,361
1988	4,800	2005	9,281
1989	4,610	2006	8,684
1990	4,548	2007	8,471
1991	4,123	2008	6,381
1992	4,629	2009	4,945
1993	5,351	2010	5,324 est.
1994	6,033		

Sources: U.S. Department of Energy (2010).

Table 8.7 ADJUSTED INCOME STATEMENT FOR METAL BROTHERS, INC.

	2010	2011	2012	2013	2014	2015	2016
Revenues:							
Patent Licensing Fees	$0	$0	$250,000	$350,000	$500,000	$650,000	$800,000
Operating Expenses:							
Cost of Goods	36,000	36,000	36,000	36,000	36,000	36,000	36,000
Owner's Compensation	0	0	0	100,000	100,000	100,000	100,000
Other Salaries	12,000	12,000	15,000	20,000	20,000	20,000	20,000
Payroll Taxes	1,250	1,250	1,300	10,300	10,300	10,300	10,300
Profit Sharing Plan	0	0	0	0	0	0	0

Misc. Supplies	2,000	2,000	2,000	2,000	2,000	2,000	2,000
Depreciation	800	800	800	800	800	800	800
Rent	24,000	24,000	24,000	24,000	24,000	24,000	24,000
Insurance	9,000	9,000	9,000	9,000	9,000	9,000	9,000
Other Expenses	3,000	3,000	3,000	3,000	3,000	3,000	3,000
Total Operating Expenses	$88,050	$88,050	$91,100	$205,100	$205,100	$205,100	$205,100
Net Earnings (Net Income)	($88,050)	($88,050)	$158,900	$144,900	$294,900	$444,900	$594,900

- A 25 percent discount rate is assumed.
- Normalized owner's compensation is assumed to be $100,000 per year, and thus adjusted net earnings are as shown in Table 8.7.
- A 1–1–1–1–1–1 weighting scheme is assumed.

Based on these assumptions and the data in Table 8.7, the present value of adjusted future net earnings as of the beginning of 2011 is $659,963. A zero percent marketability discount is assumed

Table 8.8 PRESENT VALUE OF ADJUSTED FUTURE NET EARNINGS VALUATION METHOD

Steps	Procedure
1	Determine the expected life of the business—a limited life of n years or an indefinite life.
2	Estimate an appropriate discount rate, r.
3	Normalize the Income Statement.
4	Calculate a weighted average of adjusted future net earnings, assuming that a weighted average of adjusted future net earnings is appropriate.
5	Calculate the present value of the weighted average of adjusted future net earnings using either the limited life present value equation (4.1), to which a residual value for the business must then be added, or the capitalization equation (4.2).
6	Adjust for marketability as appropriate.

because the Metal brothers own the patent to the production of the aluminum alloy and because the automobile manufactures face a 2020 deadline to meet the 35 miles per gallon fuel standard.

8.4 SUMMARY

Here is our punch line. The critical aspect of the valuation of Metal Brothers, Inc. is the valuator's knowledge about the underlying trends in the complementary technologies. In other words, absent information about new safety devices being researched through the support of the U.S. Department of Energy, and absent information about when these complementary technologies would be commercialized and installed on new vehicles, any effort to value Metal Brothers, Inc. would have been, in our opinion, speculative.

Although the example of Metal Brothers, Inc. in this chapter is semi-hypothetical, and by that we mean that the financial data were constructed for illustrative purposes based on known and observable information, the point is simple. Traditional valuation approaches are limited and even misleading when applied to an entrepreneurial enterprise, as we have defined one. The key is to focus on and understand the availability of alternative or complementary technologies.

NOTES

1   Some of the information presented here for illustrative purposes is based on factual data and other information is based on conjecture for emphasizing our methodology.
2   This Act was originally called the Clean Energy Act of 2007.
3   For greater detail about CAFÉ standards, see Yacobussi and Bamberger (2008).

4   It was common knowledge at the time the Metal brothers founded their company that the Lightweighting Materials' (LMs') component of the U.S. Department of Energy's Vehicle Technologies Program was involved in research related to advanced materials. According to Das: "To achieve its long-term goal, LM has prioritized its research areas in several lightweighting material including advanced high-strength steel, *aluminum* [emphasis added], magnesium, titanium, and composites" (2009, p. 1).

5   See U.S. Department of Energy (2010).

Concluding Statement

We began this book with a statement about who the entrepreneur is and why his or her contribution to the economy is not only unique but also crucial. Some of the greatest economic thinkers of all time have answered the question of who the entrepreneur is. Relying heavily on the ideas of Schumpeter, Machlup, and others, we concluded that the entrepreneur is one who perceives an opportunity and has the ability to act on that opportunity. We went on to say in the introductory chapter that for our purposes it does not matter whether the entrepreneur provoked the change that created the opportunity or simply perceived that it existed. Either way, action implies that the entrepreneur had the courage to embrace risk in the face of uncertainty. And thus, an entrepreneurial enterprise is the manifestation of the entrepreneur's perception and action. We then delimited an entrepreneurial enterprise to be one that is technology based and has yet to generate revenues.

Scholars have also identified why the entrepreneur makes an invaluable contribution to the economic well-being of society. By creating and growing a new firm, the entrepreneur provides the vehicle for getting ideas that might otherwise lie dormant into the market. The entrepreneur serves as an agent of change and innovative activity in an economy where innovation is the force underlying economic growth, jobs, and a sustainable standard of living.

Careful studies have uncovered a positive relationship between entrepreneurship and innovative activity. Where there are more entrepreneurs, there is also more innovation, job creation, and economic growth.

In light of the key role played by new entrepreneurial and technology-based firms, and their importance to economic growth and development, it was a next logical step in this book to ask how one values an entrepreneurial enterprise.[1] We started with the premise that the application of traditional approaches to the valuation of small entrepreneurial enterprises is wanting in several respects because traditional valuation methods are modeled in a manner that is applicable to a going-concern business that has a history of sales and revenues. That is not the case for an entrepreneurial enterprise. Through argument and example, we made the point that when valuing an entrepreneurial enterprise, the key is to focus on and understand the availability of alternative or complementary technologies. Two chapters are devoted specifically to numerically illustrating our point of view.

Where does one take our point of view from here? We are convinced that the general issue of valuing an entrepreneurial enterprise is of great and growing importance. In the era of globalization, creating and acting upon new ideas to generate products and services that are valuable in the market has taken on a new significance. The production of goods and services based on established ideas and ways of doing things tends to be outsourced and offshored to less expensive locations. Consumers will continue to want standardized products and services. However, those goods and services will be increasingly supplied by companies located in low-cost places, such as Southeast Asia, India, and China. This means that those companies in high-cost locations, such as North America and Europe, are going to be involved in the creation and commercialization of new ideas that have not yet been successfully developed anywhere else, which suggests that entrepreneurial firms will become more the norm than the exception in the future.

As new entrepreneurial firms are born there will be a greater need for valuation. Some of these firms will die off, hence the need for insight regarding how one determines a liquidation value on an enterprise that has yet to blossom but has transferable intellectual property. Some of these firms will need outside funding, from a venture capitalist perhaps, and others will be purchased by other domestic or international firms. Regardless, valuation becomes the linchpin to deal with before the firm can figuratively and literally move on. And, of course, some of these firms will survive and prosper. They, too, will eventually need a fair market valuation to secure additional financial resources or merge with other firms.

We believe that this book is a first step toward a more appropriate and enlightened way to think about valuing an entrepreneurial enterprise. We expect that those versed in—or, should we say, entrenched in—traditional approaches to valuation will say that our first step is a baby step. Perhaps it is, and we are truthfully not concerned about the size of the step. In our ever-changing technology-based environment, awareness of complementary technologies is key to not only approaching valuations but also to thinking about efficiency through the integration of equipment and even ideas.

NOTES

1   We motivated much of the discussion in this book on the basis of the number of entrepreneurial enterprises potentially in need of valuation. However, there is another side to the coin that we have not discussed, namely the growing visibility of entrepreneurial enterprises brought about by their economic importance.

In the United States productivity growth fell during the early 1970s and again during the late 1970s and early 1980s, as it did in many industrialized nations. The evidence shows that total factor productivity growth during the late 1960s and early 1970s was less than one-half that of previous decades. While there have been many ex post explanations for the slowdown, such as the OPEC oil crisis in 1973 and industry's slow adjustment to it, there seems to have been a general agreement at that time and shortly thereafter that public policy aimed at stimulating innovation would be effective for stimulating economic growth. To wit, the Bayh-Dole Act was passed in 1980, and the R&E tax credit was passed in 1981.

In addition to the broad-based emphasis on innovation (i.e., the diffusion of patented technologies and the increase in R&D investments from these two legislative initiatives), a research report from MIT's *Neighborhood and Regional Change* program was independently and coincidently published in 1979. Birch (1979, 1981) concluded in that report that three-fifths of the net new jobs between 1969 and 1976 were created by small firms with 20 or fewer employees. According to Birch, "On average about 60 percent of all jobs in the U.S. are generated by firms with 20 or fewer employees, about 50 percent of all jobs are created by independent, small entrepreneurs. Large firms (those with over 500 employees) generate less than 15 percent of all net new jobs" (1979, p. 29). Also, Birch (1979, 1987) reported that approximately 80% of net new jobs were created by firms with 100 or fewer employees.[1] Unbeknownst to Birch at that time, his writings would become the genesis for a new research field related to the economics of small businesses.

One might think of the productivity recovery that began in the early 1980s in terms of entrepreneurial responses to disequilibria. Or, using the terms of Audretsch (2007) and Audretsch and Thurik (2001, 2004), the recovery from the productivity slowdown reflects the end of the era of the managed economy (with predictable outputs coming from an established manufacturing sector) and the emergence of the entrepreneurial economy.

In the entrepreneurial economy, characterized by the emergence of economic agents embodied with entrepreneurial capital, smaller firms have a greater ability to be innovative, or to adopt and adapt others' new technologies and ideas, and thus quickly and efficiently appropriate investments in new knowledge that are made externally. Entrepreneurial capital engenders growth in new enterprises, and enterprise growth augments economic growth. In addition, entrepreneurial capital provides diversity among firms. According to Audretsch and Thurik, "entrepreneurship has emerged [during the late 1970s] as the engine of economic and social development throughout the world" (2004, p. 144). As a result, it is perhaps not surprising that policymakers toward the end of the 1970s embraced small firms as engines of future economic growth.

Carlsson (1992) offered two explanations for this shift in policy emphasis toward small, entrepreneurial firms. First, there had been a fundamental
change in the world economy beginning in the mid-1970s. Global competition was increasing, markets were becoming fragmented, and the determi-
nants of future economic growth were uncertain. Thus, entrepreneurial
leadership adjusted to this disequilibrium. Second, flexible automation was
being introduced throughout the manufacturing sector, thus reducing economies of scale as a barrier for entry into many markets and thereby opening
the door for smaller, entrepreneurial firms to enter and succeed.

REFERENCES

Acs, Z. J., and P. Mueller. 2008. "Employment effects and business dynamics: Mice, gazelles and elephants." *Small Business Economics* 30: 85–100.

Atkinson, R. D. and D. B. Audretsch. 2010. "Economic doctrines and innovation policy." *Innovations* 5: 163–206.

Audretsch, D. B. 1995. *Innovation and Industry Evolution*. Cambridge: MIT Press.

Audretsch, D. B. 2007. *The Entrepreneurial Society*. New York: Oxford University Press.

Audretsch, D. B. and M. Keilbach. 2007. "The theory of knowledge spillover entrepreneurship." *Journal of Management Studies* 44: 1242–1254.

Audretsch, D. B., M. Keilbach, and E. Lehmann. 2006. *Entrepreneurship and Economic Growth*. New York: Oxford University Press.

Audretsch, D. B. and A. R. Thurik. 2001. "What's new about the new economy? From the managed to the entrepreneurial economy." *Industrial and Corporate Change* 10: 17–34.

Audretsch, D. B. and A. R. Thurik. 2004. "The model of the entrepreneurial economy." *International Journal of Entrepreneurship Education* 2: 143–166.

Baumol, W. 1968. "Entrepreneurship in economic theory." *American Economic Review* 58: 64–71.

Bayh, B. (2004). Introductory statement of Birch Bayh, September 13, 1978, cited from the Association of University Technology Managers Report, Recollections: Celebrating the History of AUTM and the Legacy of Bayh–Dole, Washington, DC, Association of University Technology Managers.

Birch, D. L. 1979. "The job generation process." Unpublished report, MIT Program on *Neighborhood and Regional Change*.

Birch, D. L. 1981. "Who creates jobs?" *Public Interest* 65: 3–14.

Birch, D. L. 1987. *Job Creation in America: How Our Smallest Companies Put the Most People to Work.* New York: The Free Press.

Blinder, A. S. 1987. *Soft hearts: Tough-minded Economics for a Just Society.* Reading, MA: Addison-Wesley.

Bresnahan, T. and A. Gambardella. 2004. *Building High-tech Clusters: Silicon Valley and Beyond.* Cambridge: Cambridge University Press.

Carlsson, B. 1992. "The rise of small business: causes and consequences," in *Singular Europe: Economy and Policy of the European Community after 1992.* Edited by W. J. Adams. Ann Arbor: University of Michigan Press.

Case, J. 1992. *From the Ground Up: The Resurgence of American Entrepreneurship.* New York: Simon & Schuster.

Das, S. 2009. "Cost-effectiveness of a 40% body and chassis weight-reduction goal in light-duty vehicles." Oak Ridge, TN: Oak Ridge National Laboratory for the U.S. Department of Energy.

Dean, J., A. Browne, and S. Oster. 2010. "China, state capitalism sparks a global backlash." *Wall Street Journal,* November 16.

Economists 1989. "The rise and rise of America's small firms (small business grows)", *The Economist* (US), (Business), January 21, 1989, pp. 173–174.

Friedman, M. and R. Friedman. 1979. *Free to Choose.* New York: Mariner Books.

Hébert, R. F. and A. N. Link. 1988. *The Entrepreneur: Mainstream Views and Radical Critiques.* New York: Praeger.

Hébert, R. F. and A. N. Link. 2009. *A History of Entrepreneurship.* London: Routledge.

Keynes, J. M. 1935. *The General Theory of Employment, Interest, and Money.* London: Routledge.

Krugman, P. 1990. *The Age of Diminished Expectations.* Cambridge, MA: MIT Press.

Laffer, A. B. 2004. "The Laffer curve: past, present and future." Laffer Associates, January 6.

Link, A. N. 1992. "Economic impacts of NIST-supported standards for the U.S. optical fiber industry: 1981—present." Final report prepared for the Center for Electronics and Electrical Engineering, Washington, DC: National Institute of Standards and Technology.

Link, A. N., and M. B. Boger. 1999. *The Art and Science of Business Valuation.* New York: Quorum Publishers.

Link, A. N. and J. T. Scott. 2010. "Employment growth from the Small Business Innovation Research Program." *Small Business Economics,* Online First™.

McCraw, T. K., 2007. *Prophet of Innovation: Joseph Schumpeter and Creative Destruction.* Cambridge, MA: Belknap Press.

Machlup, F. 1980. *Knowledge and Knowledge Production.* Princeton, NJ: Princeton University Press.

Mandel, M. 2004. *Rational Exuberance: Silencing the Enemies of Growth*. New York: Harper Collins.

Mankiw, G. 2004. Ask the White House. http://ia410331.us.archive.org/peth04/20041020115643/http://www.whitehouse.gov/ask/20041008.html

Mason, M. K. 2010. Worldwide business startups. http://www.moyak.com/papers/business-startups-entrepreneurs.html

Mowery, D. 2005. "The Bayh-Dole Act and high-technology entrepreneurship in U.S. universities: chick, egg, or something else?" Paper presented at the Eller Centre Conference on Entrepreneurship Education and Technology Transfer, University of Arizona.

Nollsch, J. 2010. "Valuation is a tricky subject for early-stage entrepreneurs raising capital." http://angelcapitalsummit.org/blog/valuation-tricky-subject-for-early-stage-entrepreneurs-raising-capital.

Oak Ridge National Laboratory. 2010. *Transportation Energy Data Book: Edition 29*. Oak Ridge, TN: Oak Ridge National Laboratory for the U.S. Department of Energy.

Orszag, P. R. 2001. "Marginal tax rate reductions and the economy: what would be the long-term effects of the Bush tax cut?" Washington, DC: Center on Budget and Policy Priorities.

Prodi, R. 2002. "For a new European entrepreneurship." Public speech, Instituto de Empresa in Madrid.

Robert Morris Associates. *Annual Statement Studies*. Philadelphia: Robert Morris Associates.

Reynolds, P. D. and R. T. Curtin. 2008. "Business creation in the United States: panel study of entrepreneurial dynamics II initial assessment." *Foundation and Trends in Entrepreneurship* 4: 155–307.

Scherer, F. M. 1970. *Industrial Market Structure and Economic Performance*. Chicago: Rand McNally.

Scherer, F. M. 1992. "Schumpeter and plausible capitalism." *Journal of Economic Literature* 30: 1416-1433.

Schultz, T. W. 1975. "The value of the ability to deal with disequilibria." *Journal of Economic Literature* 13: 827–846.

Schumpeter, J. A. 1911. *Theorie der wirtschaftlichen Entwicklung*. Berlin: Duncker und Humblot.

Schumpeter, J. A. 1939. *Business Cycles*. New York: McGraw-Hill.

Schumpeter, J. A. 1942. *Capitalism, Socialism and Democracy*. New York: Harper.

Schumpeter, J. A. 1950. "The march into socialism." *American Economic Review* 40: 446-456.

Schumpeter, J. A. 1928. "The instability of capitalism." *Economic Journal* 38: 361–386.

Schumpeter, J. A. 1934. *The Theory of Economic Development*. Cambridge: Harvard University Press.

Smith, A. 1776 (2000). *The Wealth of Nations*. New York: Penguin Classics.

Solow, R. 1956. "A contribution to the theory of economic growth." *Quarterly Journal of Economics* 70, 65-94.

U. S. Census Bureau. 2007. *2007 Economic Census*. Washington, DC: Government Printing Office.

U. S. Census Bureau. 2009. *Statistical Abstract of the United States: 2009*. Washington, DC: Government Printing Office.

U.S. Department of Transportation. 2003. *Vehicle Weight, Fatality Risk and Crash Compatibility of Model Year 1991–99 Passenger Cars and Light Trucks*. Washington, DC: U.S. Department of Transportation.

U. S. Small Business Administration. 2009. *The Small Business Economy: A Report to the President*. Washington, DC: Government Printing Office.

U.S. Small Business Administration, Office of Advocacy. 2010. Frequently asked questions. www.sba.gov/advo.Wallsten, S. J. 2004. "The role of government in regional technology development: The effects of public venture capital and science parks," in *Building High-tech Clusters: Silicon Valley and Beyond*. Edited by T. Bresnahan and A. Gambardella. Cambridge: Cambridge University Press, 229–279.

Yacobussi, B. D. and R. Bamberger. 2008. *Automobile and Light Truck Fuel Economy: The CAFÉ Standards*. CRS Report to Congress. Washington, DC: Government Printing Office.

INDEX